The Conservative Tradition in America

The Conservative Tradition
in America

ALLEN GUTTMANN

1967

OXFORD UNIVERSITY PRESS

NEW YORK

For Britt, Erika Britt, and Betty

Preface

Authors hope their books will be read from first page to last, and know that many readers have time merely to consult a chapter or to use the index. This book was conceived and written as a whole, but chapters and sections (some of them published previously in somewhat different form) are meant to make sense in themselves. My plea to the reader of a single section is simple. After the Introduction, which defines terms, "Conservatism" and "Liberalism" are used substantively; they refer to historically identifiable ideologies in which attitudes toward change are but a single component. If this usage is familiar to him, I have no further plea; if it is not, I urge that he read the Introduction first.

For permission to draw upon earlier versions of several chapters of this book, I am grateful to the editors of *American Literature, American Quarterly, The American Scholar, The Kenyon Review,* and *The New England Quarterly.* Specific references are given in the text. I am also grateful to President Calvin H. Plimpton of Amherst College for the Trustee Fellowship during which much of the research was done, and to Sheldon Meyer and Caroline Taylor of Oxford University Press for indispensable editorial assistance. Among my colleagues, I wish especially to thank Theodore Baird and Benjamin DeMott, from whom I have received specific criticisms, and Theodore Greene, Hugh Hawkins, George Kateb, N. Gordon Levin, Leo Marx, Bruce Morgan, Edwin C. Rozwenc, and John William Ward, with whom I have worked in Amherst's American Studies courses. They, and other colleagues, are largely responsible for whatever education I have received since I departed from graduate school. If this book indicates that I have not learned enough, the blame is mine and not theirs. They tried.

A. G.

Amherst, Massachusetts
June 1967

Contents

The Conservative Tradition in America

Liberalism and the Political Theory of Edmund Burke

From the 1770's to the 1960's, from the Committees of Correspondence to the civil rights movement, American political rhetoric has remained remarkably constant. Liberty and equality have been our watchwords. Although each generation of reformers discovers in anger that rhetoric is not the only form of reality and that political ideals are at best imperfectly institutionalized, the Liberal tradition (of which John Locke is *fons* if not *origo*) has dominated American political thought and, to a much lesser degree, political behavior.* Almost free of the vestiges of feudalism, protected by two vast oceans, nourished by natural and then by technological abundance, America has flourished and Liberalism has grown unaccustomed to opposition. American Liberals, unused to serious intellectual challenges from Right and Left,

---

* In order to reduce some of the confusion that has been characteristic of discussions of the key terms of this book, I shall use "Liberalism" and "Conservatism," with initial capitals, to refer always to the political traditions derived from John Locke and from Edmund Burke. I shall follow the same policy with "Liberal" and "Conservative." The terms "liberalism" and "conservatism," and their derivatives, will be used as discussed in this introductory chapter—i.e. to indicate two different attitudes toward change. Quotations have been altered to. conform to this usage.

have often been unable to cope with unfamiliar modes of social organization. This inability has, in addition, led to a lack of clarity about Liberalism itself. "The ironic flaw in American Liberalism lies in the fact that we have never had a real Conservative tradition." [1] This comment by Louis Hartz is, like the book from which it is taken, an overstatement, but it touches an important truth. Ideas are defined in the context of other ideas; undefined ideas are liable to be poor guides for the conduct of political affairs, domestic as well as foreign.

Conservatism stands in opposition to Liberalism, but the dominance (in America) of the latter has meant that the former is often misunderstood. In the wrangle of partisan debate and in the polemics of electoral campaigns, "conservative" signifies an attitude toward social change: the conservative cherishes the status quo and defends established institutions against those who seek to transform them. "The essence of conservatism," writes Samuel P. Huntington, "is the passionate affirmation of the value of existing institutions." [2] Willmoore Kendall agrees: "In any given time and place conservatives are those who [defend] an established order against those who seek to undermine or transform it." [3]

Barry Goldwater is clearly this kind of conservative; on a much higher intellectual level, Friedrich von Hayek is this kind of conservative. What these very dissimilar men have in common is an outspoken attachment to nineteenth-century Liberalism in general and to the doctrines of laissez-faire economics in particular. They are *conservative* Liberals who seek to carry on in our time the tradition of which Thomas Jefferson, John Stuart Mill, and Alexis de Tocqueville are notable nineteenth-century exemplars.* Hayek understands and laments this usage of "conservative." His stand against all forms of collectivism is made in the name of Liberalism. Noting the confusion of American discussions, he writes, "I will nevertheless continue for the moment to describe as Lib-

---

* A minor irony: this usage of "conservative" is typically Liberal in that it assumes in the form of the definition that attitudes toward change are the defining characteristics of social groups.

eral the position which I hold and which I believe differs as much from true Conservatism as from socialism." [4]

As Hayek's comment suggests, any effort at transatlantic analysis will be confused if the analyst forgets that the terms "Liberalism" and "Conservatism" have kept much of their nineteenth-century significance in Europe. But even within the American context popular usage is frequently befuddled by a failure to realize that change is seldom uniform throughout a society. The affirmation of individual liberty in religion is said to be "liberal"; the affirmation of individual liberty in economics is said to be "conservative"; both were part of the nineteenth-century Liberal's program of opposition to all forms of coercive authority. Empirical studies based on this kind of popular usage are often skewed into inanity. In constructing a scale for Liberalism that actually tests Liberalism in politics and religion, socialism in economics, and lack of discrimination in aesthetics, one contributor to the *Journal of Social Psychology,* blind to the beam in his own eye, discovered that his subjects held inconsistent views. [5]

Historians too have written as if they were unaware of the historical dimension implicit in the popular definitions of "conservative" and "liberal." Robert McCloskey, in his well-known study of William Graham Sumner, Stephen J. Field, and Andrew Carnegie, *American Conservatism in the Age of Enterprise,* identifies these men as conservative because their ideas became part of a defended status quo in social thought, in jurisprudence, and in business enterprise. But Sumner, Field, and Carnegie were innovators and reformers. They were intellectually aggressive in relation to other men who were, on the issues of that day, the conservatives. Gabriel Kolko's provocative study of big business and government legislation, *The Triumph of Conservatism,* is weakened by the same anachronistic error. It is as if historians of the twenty-first century were to characterize Eugene Debs, Norman Thomas, and Michael Harrington as conservatives because the socialism they called for had become the status quo which the twenty-first century had, in turn, successfully supplanted. To define "conservatism" as support for established institutions and to transfer the particular relationships of one's own time to previous eras is to have the worst of two semantic worlds.[6]

Attempts made by various writers to connect this relativistic conservatism of popular usage to the political theory of Edmund Burke have further muddied the already impure waters. Burke was, to be sure, a conservative in the popular sense. He upheld the inherited institutions of English society against threats from within and without. But his defense of England in 1790 has become a substantive political theory to which subsequent generations have returned in order to extract specific tenets or to adopt it in its entirety. His conservatism in the relative sense has become Conservatism in an absolute sense because of the magnitude of the challenge—the French Revolution.

M. Morton Auerbach has traced Conservatism as an ideology back as far as Plato;[7] Henry A. Kissinger and Peter Viereck have pointed to Metternich as a model of Conservative polity;[8] and Roman Catholic Conservatives have drawn from the Church's own political theorists.[9] But Englishmen and Americans turn most often to Burke's political philosophy for an ideal type (in Max Weber's terms), for a "model" by which social reality can be tested.[10] It is Conservatism as an ideology, as a body of interrelated political theorems, that is the primary subject of this book. The men and women who followed Barry Goldwater in 1964 will reappear only that they may be distinguished from other men and women dedicated to an earlier ideology.

Burke's references to the Glorious Revolution of 1688 are laudatory, but he had little to say of the English Revolution of the 1640's. He was sympathetic to a certain amount of laissez-faire in economics, but he advocated state intervention in economic affairs and urged Parliament to abolish the slave trade, to establish mercantile monopolies, to give subsidies and bounties, and to curb the immense power of the East India Company.[11] He decried the encroachments of the crown upon the rights of Parliament in *Thoughts on the Cause of the Present Discontents* (1770), but he became increasingly friendly to monarchy. He was convinced that conciliatory measures were necessary to end the dispute with the colonies, but the French Revolution settled all doubts—or should have settled them—about Burke's fundamental commitments. He was completely antagonistic not merely to the consequences of the French Revolution, which many Liberals deplored, but also to the Liberal doctrines set forth in Locke's *Treatises* on government and proclaimed in the Declaration of the Rights of Man. Whether or not one agrees with Ernest Barker that Burke's thought changed between the 1770's and the 1790's, one must concede that *Reflections on the Revolution in France* is a comprehensive denial of Lockean thought.[12]

Dr. Richard Price, a Liberal minister, was the immediate cause of Burke's reflections. Price preached to the Revolutionary Society of London a sermon in praise of the French Revolution. He asserted three rights (which Burke quoted in his reply):

> To choose our own governors,
> To cashier them for misconduct,
> To frame a government for ourselves.

Burke denied all three. "So far is it from being true that we acquired a right by the [Glorious] Revolution to elect our kings, that, if we had possessed it before, the English nation did at that time most solemnly renounce and abdicate it, for themselves, and for all their posterity forever." The king, asserted Burke in accents far different from those of earlier speeches, is the nation's sovereign and not its servant. To talk of rightful revolution is nonsense, and to talk of a new government is fantastic. "The very idea of the fabrication of a new government is enough to fill us with disgust and horror."

Liberty and equality, as understood by Liberals, are rejected as decisively as the right of revolution and the right to renew the social contract. In a letter written in October of 1789, Burke had insisted that liberty "is not solitary, unconnected, individual, selfish liberty, as if every man was to regulate the whole of his conduct by his own will. The liberty I mean is *social* freedom. It is that state of things in which liberty is secured by the equality of restraint." He continued to emphasize "social freedom" in his *Reflections,* where he praised "a manly, moral, regulated liberty" that can be "combined with government, with public force, with the discipline and obedience of armies. . . ." Burke in his earlier career had not ignored individual liberties, but he grew ever more interested in restraint of these liberties. The "inclinations of men should frequently be thwarted, their will controlled, and their passions brought into subjection. . . . The restraints on men, as well as their liberties, are to be reckoned among their rights."

One test of liberty is the relation of the individual citizen to the state. Liberalism tends toward philosophical anarchism (which William Godwin reached, in *Political Justice,* in 1793), toward a praise of civil disobedience and the sort of government which governs not at all. For this interpretation of individual liberty, Burke had very harsh words:

> To avoid . . . the evils of inconstancy and versatility, ten thousand times worse than those of obstinacy and the blindest prejudice, we have consecrated the state, that no man should approach to look into its defects or corruptions but with due caution; that he should never dream of beginning its reformation by its subversion; that he should approach to the faults of the state as to the wounds of a father, with pious awe and trembling solicitude.

The tone is closer to Robert Filmer's *Patriarcha* than to the *Treatise* Locke wrote against Filmer's "divine-right" support of monarchy. It is difficult to disagree with Alfred Cobban's imagistic judgment: "Burke spent his life on his knees before the great mystery of social life." [13]

Against the ideal of equality, Burke was equally vehement. He held forth the ideal of hierarchy. Those "who attempt to level never equalize. In all societies consisting of various descriptions of citizens, some descriptions must be uppermost. The levellers only change and pervert the natural order of things." The emo-

tive power behind the principles emerges in Burke's lamentation
for the royal victims of the Revolution. In the revolutionary
"scheme of things, a king is but a man, a queen is but a woman,
a woman is but an animal. . . . The murder of a king, or a
queen, or a bishop, or a father, are only common homicide." His
effusive tributes to Marie Antoinette, cut down by the "swinish
multitude," culminate in a *cri de coeur:*

> I thought ten thousand swords must have leaped from their
> scabbards to avenge even a look that threatened her with in-
> sult. But the age of chivalry is gone. That of sophisters, econo-
> mists, and calculators has succeeded; and the glory of Europe
> is extinguished forever. Never, never more, shall we behold
> that generous loyalty to rank and sex, that proud submission,
> that dignified obedience, that subordination of the heart. . . .
> The unbought grace of life, the cheap defence of nations, the
> nurse of manly sentiment and heroic enterprise, is gone!

Pages of sentences like these stirred Tom Paine, in *The Rights of
Man,* to a satirical retort: "He pities the plumage but forgets the
dying bird." *

Liberal politics has its philosophical base in the Lockean conviction that human reason can be trusted to discover Nature's
laws, moral as well as physical. Burke, who reserved his most ex-
cremental metaphors for the "sophisters" and metaphysicians who
presumed to speculate on political principles, preferred the wisdom of experience to rational inquiry. He urged reliance on "the
general bank and capital of nations and of ages." His discussion
of the alleged abjuration of rights at the time of the Glorious
Revolution emphasizes the prescriptive nature of historical experience. "We have an inheritable crown, an inheritable peerage,
and a House of Commons and a people inheriting privileges,

---

* Burke's sycophancy appears in an early letter to the Duke of Richmond
(November 17, 1772): ". . . we [commoners] creep on the ground, we belly
into melons that are exquisite for size and flavour, yet still are but annual plants,
that perish with our season, and leave no sort of traces behind. . . . You . . .
are in my eye the great oaks that shade a country, and perpetuate your benefits
from generation to generation."

franchises, and liberties from a long line of ancestors." In his contempt for the theory of natural rights, Burke "bows before the pageant of history and worships its sanctities."[14] At moments, Burke seems to make antiquity the only source of value: "We procure reverence to our civil institutions on the principle upon which Nature teaches us to revere individual men: on account of their age, and on account of those from whom they are descended."

Against Burke's sense of the past, one can set Jefferson's belief that the earth belongs always to the living, or Emerson's rejection of the past in favor of the glory of the present moment. Here, for instance, is the opening of *Nature*:

> Our age is retrospective. It builds the sepulchres of the fathers. It writes biographies, histories, and criticism. The foregoing generations beheld God and nature face to face; we, through their eyes. Why should not we also enjoy an original relation to the universe? . . . The sun shines today also. There is more wool and flax in the fields. There are new lands, new men, new thoughts. Let us demand our own works and laws and worship.

Burke's efforts to legitimize the status quo did not stop with the appeal to history. Recent scholarship has amply demonstrated the Christian basis of his political thought. Peter J. Stanlis, with the encouragement of Russell Kirk, has transformed Burke into the Complete Christian Philosopher: "Burke had an encyclopedic knowledge of the tradition of Natural Law in Western thought" which he always appealed to in every important political situation. "What is more, by Natural Law Burke always meant the same thing, and he applied it as the ultimate test of justice and liberty in human affairs."[15] This formulation seems to venture beyond the evidence, but it does suggest what Burke's most ardent admirers most admire in him. Like lesser Conservatives, Burke often assumed that history and Providence were one, that the institutions of his own society were divinely sanctioned. Listening to the thunderclap of Revelation and to the reiterated wisdom of

generations past, Burke never heard the appeal to reason made by
Locke and by the *philosophes* of the Enlightenment.

The influence of Edmund Burke on America has been much
debated. Clinton Rossiter, whose *Conservatism in America* remains the best introduction to the problem, is certain that Conservatism has never been of much moment in the United States,
at least not since the time of the demise of the Federalist party.

> Those Americans who speak and write as genuine, self-con-
> scious Conservatives are today, as they have been for more
> than a century, an eccentric minority in the world of ideas, a
> misunderstood minority in the world of right-wing politics.[16]

Russell Kirk, on the other hand, is sure that "Burke's American
influence has been incalculably pervasive," and Willmoore Kendall thinks that "in the decisive dimension, the 'Burkeens,' British
and American, have had their way." The great majority of scholars agree with Rossiter, but Kirk and Kendall are not wholly
wrong.[17] While it is certainly true that a political party committed
to Burkean Conservatism is almost unthinkable at the present
moment, it is nonetheless a fact that Conservatism has persisted
in America as *an essentially literary phenomenon*. Pushed in disarray from the battlefield of political activity, Conservatism has
taken refuge in the citadel of ideas. The democratization of
American society has made Conservatism increasingly feeble as
an institutionalized force, but the Conservative's dream of a hier-
archically structured society of prescribed values and restrained
liberty has continued on as an important and usually unrecog-
nized aspect of American literature. The intellectual tradition of
socialism is far more important than the electoral weight of the
Socialist party; similarly, Conservative novelists and poets, essay-
ists, critics, and philosophers have a place in our literary history
to which they could not have aspired had they depended on the
popularity of their attitudes.

Looking for Conservatism, historians with a political orienta-
tion have seldom looked at literature. And literary critics and

historians, intent upon the "Americanness" of our classic writers, have given insufficient attention to Conservative elements in the canonical authors. Occasional essays have pointed to the largely literary basis of the New Conservatism,[18] and specialists have written well on the Conservatism of one or another American author, but no one has outlined in sufficient detail a Conservative tradition in its social and political context.[19] No one has done what Raymond Williams did in *Culture and Society* for Conservatism in England, for the literary tradition that includes Burke, Coleridge, Carlyle, Ruskin, Arnold, and T. S. Eliot.

My intention is *not* a refutation of the errors of Conservatism, for M. Morton Auerbach, David Spitz, and numerous others have done this capably.[20] Nor is it my intention to provide a complete history of American Conservatism, or even to say all that can be said about the men and books discussed. My primary purpose is to trace the decline of Conservatism in American political life, the continuation of Conservatism in American literature, and the paths taken by various writers in their attempt to revive Conservatism in the twentieth century. My secondary purpose is to indicate why certain men and movements are *not* as Conservative as they are sometimes claimed to be.

For a problem as protean as that of Conservatism, a variety of procedures seems useful. Chapter I, which moves from the 1760's to the 1860's, is an analysis of political ideas and attitudes with what I hope is proper attention to their institutional context. The Tories, the Federalists, and the "Cavaliers" of the plantation South are the *dramatis personae*. Chapter II represents a different approach. The focus is on literary images and what they imply. Crucial here is the image of the ancestral mansion as one locus of a traditional order. Chapters III and IV are concerned with institutions rather than with images; the first is devoted to the church and the second to the military establishment. Chapter V returns to a chronological organization and traces the fortunes of Conservatism from the days of Henry Adams to those of John Crowe Ransom and Allen Tate. The last chapter is an attempt to map the contemporary scene and to propagandize, a little, for my own preferences.

Compared to the ineffable richness of life as it is actually lived, the most complicated and subtle of books resembles a radar screen. Radar reduces complexity to a blip, but it is, nonetheless, a device which enables us, sometimes, to make the crude distinctions upon which our lives depend.

I

The Decline of American Conservatism

1 The Loyalists and the Revolution

Fifteen years before the publication of *Reflections on the Revolution in France,* the men and women who were likely to have been Burke's most attentive American readers began to depart from these tumultuous shores. Nearly 100,000 Loyalists left before, during, and immediately after the American Revolution. In proportion to the total population, they were five times as numerous as the *emigrées* of the 1790's.[1] Although men of modest fortunes departed along with colonial governors and eminent divines, the Loyalists were drawn very largely from the top of the socio-economic pyramid. They were wealthy merchants, professional men, and officials—in an age when American society was overwhelmingly agrarian. Of 76 Loyalists who were banished by New Hampshire in 1778, 30 were listed in the official records as "Gentlemen and Esquires."[2] Governor John Wentworth was, of course, among them. In Massachusetts, only 11 per cent of the Loyalists who, after the war, sought reimbursement for their losses were farmers, and statistics for the other states indicate the Loyalists were what everyone at the time knew they were—the most "substantial" men in the colonies.

They were replaced by men drawn in part from the same social stratum and in part from somewhat lower strata. The current historical debate over the American Revolution as a social movement commenced in 1909, when Carl Becker commented that the question of home rule was complicated by the additional question: Who shall rule at home? [3] An elementary fact, often obscured by the welter of charts and tables of social status, is that the Loyalists disagreed with the political ideas and allegiances of the radicals. The Loyalists were, to put the matter simply, Conservatives before the French Revolution because the American Revolution was, in its ideals if not in its outcome, the forerunner of, and in some ways the model for, the greater, more bloody, more consequential revolution that began in 1789.

In the chilly climate of the Cold War, revisionist historians have labored to distinguish the American Revolution from the French, and even to deny that there had been a revolution at all. Indeed, if there *had* been, it must certainly have been a "conservative" one, perhaps "a conservative restoration of colonial prerogatives." [4] R. R. Palmer's two-volume comparative analysis, *The Age of the Democratic Revolution,* is an authoritative refutation of this revisionism. His view is that

> there was a real revolution in America, and . . . it was a painful conflict, in which many were injured. . . . It is my belief also, John Quincy Adams notwithstanding, that the American and the French revolutions "proceeded from the same principles." The difference is that these principles were much more deeply rooted in America, and that contrary or competing principles, monarchist or aristocratic or feudal or ecclesiastical, though not absent from America, were, in comparison to Europe, very weak. . . . The American Revolution was, indeed, a movement to conserve what already existed. It was hardly, however, a "Conservative" movement, and it can give limited comfort to the theorists of Conservatism, for it was the weakness of Conservative forces in eighteenth-century America, not their strength, that made the American Revolution as moderate as it was.[5]

It was the political weakness of the Conservatives which led to their failure and to their loss, in the words of their most recent historian, not only of "their argument, their war, and their place in American society, but even [of] their proper place in history." [6] If the United States has been blessed with a consensus on political fundamentals, it is a consensus achieved by the forcible elimination of dissent.

The elimination of Jonathan Boucher is a case in point. Born in England in 1738, he came to America in 1759, went back to England to be ordained an Anglican priest by the Bishop of London, and returned to serve the Maryland and Virginia aristocracy. As the conflict with the mother country intensified, he preached submission, with "a pair of loaded pistols lying on the [pulpit] cushion." [7] He was, in Vernon Parrington's uncordial opinion, "the voice of seventeenth-century Cavalier England, speaking to an alien people, bred up in another philosophy of government." [8] His untimely sermons so enraged his flock that he was compelled to flee the country. The sentiments which had infuriated Virginians and Marylanders were published in London, in 1797, as *A View of the Causes and the Consequences of the American Revolution*. The book has a profuse dedication to George Washington and a rebuke to Edmund Burke: "It is beyond even Mr. Burke's abilities to shew, that, in point of principle, there is a shade of difference between the American revolution and the French rebellion." [9] There is a three-page footnote to drive the point home.

Like Burke, Boucher revered the "wisdom of those who have gone before us. . . ." Even more than Burke, Boucher emphasized the Biblical basis of Christian obedience. "The doctrine of *obedience for conscience sake* is . . . the great *corner-stone* of all good government." [10] The Ten Commandments imply "the great duty of *honouring and obeying the king, and all that are put in authority under him.* Reverently to submit ourselves to *all our governors, teachers, and spiritual pastors, and masters,* is indeed a duty so essential to the peace and happiness of the world, that

St. Paul thinks no Christian could be ignorant of it." [11] To disobey human ordinances is to disobey God. (The frequency of Boucher's italics suggest he was still trying, in the 1790's, to persuade his congregation to listen.)

Borrowing from Robert Filmer's defense of monarchy, *Patriarcha,* Boucher defined liberty as another form of submission: "To respect the laws, is to respect liberty in the only rational sense in which the term can be used; for liberty consists in a subserviency to law. . . . True liberty . . . is a liberty to do every thing that is right, and the being restrained from doing any thing that is wrong." [12] It is a definition that will be repeated by Conservatives luckier than Boucher.

There is, of course, a limit to obedience. No government has the right to compel a subject to do what is contrary to the subject's own conscience. Unfortunately for the God-fearing subject, obedience to God requires that the subject "patiently . . . submit to any penalties incurred by his disobedience to man." [13] This demanding form of resistance to injustice Boucher terms "passive obedience." [14] This is not what the signers of the Declaration of Independence had in mind.

Boucher concentrates, as was inevitable during the crisis of the 1770's, on the relationship of subject to sovereign and on the question of the true nature of liberty, but he pauses to condemn the idea of equality directly: "Man differs from man in every thing that can be supposed to lead to supremacy and subjection, *as one star differs from another star in glory."* [15] Like most other defenders of inequality, Boucher went on to insist that the call for equal rights before the law leads always to the demand for redistribution of property.

Boucher's writings have been dutifully discussed, along with those of Daniel Leonard, Samuel Seabury, and Joseph Galloway, by Moses Coit Tyler and other scholars driven by the Demon of Completeness, but Boucher has slipped from the historical memory of most educated Americans. Although his message seems nonsense, he ought to be remembered as an authentic, if somewhat exaggerated, representative of what the majority of his contemporaries were not.

Thomas Hutchinson, the last governor of Massachusetts Bay, has fared better in history because he occupied a much more important place in the colonial hierarchy and because he took the trouble to embed his political opinions in an important work of historical narrative. His sense of the past and of his relation to it is set forth in the three magisterial volumes of *The History of the Colony and Province of Massachusetts-Bay.* Hutchinson was, moreover, sufficiently in sympathy with the rebels to comprehend if not to agree with their discontents. For all his Conservatism, he was still a child of the Enlightenment.

His history of Massachusetts Bay is moderate, at least until it reaches the events in which Hutchinson was himself involved. It is no surprise to find him generous in his account of Anne Hutchinson; she was his great-great-grandmother. He had no sympathy for the Antinomians who challenged authority with claims of immediate revelations from God, but he was capable of irony at the expense of the supporters of order: "The opinionists were punished for being deluded enthusiasts. The other side were deluded also by a fond [i.e. foolish] opinion that the honor of God required them to punish his creatures for differing from themselves." [16] Roger Williams, whom one would expect to see abused for the excessive individualism of his piety, is, indeed, found culpable, but Hutchinson reminded his readers that "for forty years after, instead of shewing any revengeful resentment against the colony from which he had been banished, he seems to have been continually employed in acts of kindness and benevolence. . . ." [17] Hutchinson wrote curtly of those who persecuted the Quakers and more curtly still of the frenzy of the witchcraft trials. He condemned King James for his "daily advances towards despotism" and referred to the announcement of the ascension to the throne of William and Mary as "the most joyful news ever received in New-England." [18]

Distant in his opinions from Jonathan Boucher, Hutchinson

was nonetheless equidistant from the radicals of the Sam Adams faction, whom he maligned when he accused them of being motivated entirely by resentment and ambition. The grounds of his disagreement appear in the second volume of the history, published in 1767, after the Boston mob, in the midst of the Stamp Act controversy, had wrecked his handsome house, cut down his carefully tended fruit trees, and scattered the pages of his manuscript, and his irreplaceable documents, in the muddy street. His account of the difficulties of Governor Samuel Shute is clearly refracted by his own unhappy experiences:

> Under an absolute monarchy the people are without spirit, wear their chains despairing of freedom. . . . In a government founded upon the principle of liberty . . . we often see attempts for a greater degree of it than will consist with the established constitution, although anarchy, the greatest and worst of tyrannies may prove the consequence." [19]

His lawyer's concern with precedent and with the origins of institutions appeared in his constitutional argument for the subordination of the colonies to the authority of Parliament. Unable to imagine either independence or a divided sovereignty, Hutchinson tried to deflect his fellow colonists from a course sure to bring them into collision with English authority.

His public statements annoyed his listeners; his more impolitic ruminations on mob-rule he dispatched in a letter to England. The letter fell into the hands of Sam Adams, who read it to the Great and General Court. The text ruined Hutchinson's career:

> I never think of the measures necessary for the peace and good order of the colonies without pain; there must be an abridgment of what are called English liberties: I relieve myself by considering, that, in a remove from the state of nature to the most perfect state of government, there must be a great restraint of natural liberty: I doubt whether it is possible to project a system of government, in which a colony, 3000 miles distant, shall enjoy all the liberty of the parent state. . . . [20]

Hutchinson's contempt for the "inferior people" [21] differed in degree rather than in kind from that of others of his class who joined the Patriot side; it was his ready acceptance of diminished liberty for the colonial elite that took him into the opposite camp. The radicals might have conceded that natural liberties are of necessity circumscribed by the social compact, but they could not have assented to the proposition that the civil liberties of England ought to be greater than those of the American colonies.

Hutchinson loved his native land, but when a decision had to be made, he could not abandon the British monarchy and all that it implied in the way of stability, order, and continued pre-eminence. The result was defeat and an oblivion nearly as dark as Boucher's. Parrington paints him, with the palette of German Expressionist portraiture, as stubborn, sterile, vindictive, "cold, formal, arrogant, dogmatic, unimaginative, self-righteous. . . . In spite of his wig and scarlet broadcloth robes he was only an unintelligent politician, who served the hand that fed him." [22] The assessment is ungenerous. Most political historians have recognized that the Conservatives were a hard-pressed minority with motives no less mixed than other men's. Literary anthologies have long presented the Revolution as an allegory in which fair-haired Democrats vanquished skulky Aristocrats, but it is time for the *History of Massachusetts-Bay* to be read along with Franklin's *Autobiography* and Jefferson's *Notes on the State of Virginia.*

There is no need to multiply instances of Tory Conservatism or to become involved in the lively war of pamphlets that preceded the shots fired at Lexington and Concord. There was an authentic Conservative group in the colonies. They were a large segment of the ruling elite, but they were few indeed in comparison to the many who were anxious to shake off restraints, restless to get on with agrarian or mercantile enterprise. With neither a landed aristocracy nor an established church to support them, the Loyalists had no choice but to opt for submission to Parliament. They needed King George and his redcoats because "they held social or political opinions which could prevail in America only with British assistance." [23] The social order they hoped to make more Conservative became, with their departure, so thoroughly Liberal that it is difficult today—nearly two centuries later—to realize that before the Revolution there existed an alternative to middle-class democracy.

2 The Federalists and the Liberal Tradition

Between the Loyalists and the Federalists falls the shadow—the Revolution itself. Burke's horrified denial of the right of revolution places him forever in contrast to the men who claimed that governments are instituted among men to secure certain rights and that, "whenever any Form of Government becomes destructive of these ends, it is the Right of the People to alter or to abolish it, and to institute new Government. . . ." With a good will, the signers of the Declaration of Independence set themselves to the task that filled Burke with "disgust": the "fabrication" of new governments. Although they were closer to Burke than was the generation which followed them, they were definitely Liberals rather than Conservatives.

The Declaration is undeniably a Liberal document derived from Locke and his eighteenth-century popularizers. The Constitution moved in the direction of Conservatism in that the liberty of individuals and of the states (some of which had fallen under the sway of "giddy" majorities) was curtailed and the powers of the central government were enlarged. This much is obvious. Nonetheless, the right of a people to "fabricate" their own government is explicit in the Preamble to our social compact and in the first of the *Federalist Papers:*

> It has been frequently remarked that it seems to have been reserved to the people of this country, by their conduct and example, to decide the important question, whether societies of

men are really capable or not of establishing a good government from reflection and choice, or whether they are forever
destined to depend for their political constitutions on accident
and force.

The Founders of the Republic had put themselves in a position
where they had to answer the "important question" by an
affirmation of reflection and choice. Their motto, which appears
on the Great Seal printed on the dollar bill, was *Novus Ordo
Seclorum.* As Hannah Arendt points out, the motto was a
deliberate revision of Virgil's line in the Fourth Eclogue: *Mag-
nus Ordo Saeclorum.*[24] Was this not a boast of progress?

It is, moreover, possible to exaggerate, in the manner of
Charles Beard, the more Conservative aspects of the Constitution.
The first ten amendments add rights to a document already
containing numerous specific statements of Liberal polity—
among them a guarantee of habeas corpus, a prohibition of bills
of attainder, and a strict ban on titles of nobility. The processes
of ratification and amendment assume a somewhat qualified
majoritarianism and a degree of change—if not progress.

Clinton Rossiter's judgment of the Philadelphia Convention
is impressive because he an authority on the Conservatism which
the Founders are sometimes said to represent: "Although no one
in this sober gathering would have dreamed of invoking the
Goddess of Reason, neither would anyone have dared to proclaim that his opinions had the support of the God of Abraham
and Paul. The Convention of 1787 was highly rationalist and
even secular in spirit."[25] Joseph Charles writes that the "most
Conservative among them had views and assumptions which
would have astounded a European."[26] The Constitution was an
appropriate institutionalization of the ideals of the Declaration.
On August 26, 1792, the *Assemblée Nationale,* under Jacobin
control, elected George Washington, Alexander Hamilton, and
James Madison (but not Thomas Jefferson) honorary citizens
of France. The French understood the *Federalist Papers,* which

had just been translated, better than many Americans who have since imagined them a rejection of the principles of '76.[27]

One can, of course, acknowledge that the Founders as a group established Liberal institutions and still insist that *some* of the group preferred a more Conservative society than the one they were forced to live in. Of major figures, John Adams is clearly the most likely candidate for comparisons to Edmund Burke, comparisons which Russell Kirk, Clinton Rossiter, Peter Viereck, and other commentators have made. The alleged Conservatism of Adams deserves more detailed analysis.

The *Dissertation on the Canon and Feudal Law,* which Adams published in the form of letters to the *Boston Gazette* (1765), is dogmatically Lockean in its flourishing of natural rights "antecedent to all earthly government" and "derived from the great Legislator of the universe." [28] The essay is adolescent in its sneers at the "sanctified effluvia from episcopal fingers" and cocky in its sarcastic account of feudal law as "that dark ribaldry of hereditary, indefeasible right." [29] Adams, in later years, modified his tone but not his basic convictions. Writing to Jefferson in 1814, he put a wry question:

> Whether the God of nature shall govern the World by his own laws, or Whether Priests and Kings shall rule it by fictitious Miracles? Or, in other Words, whether Authority is originally in the People? or whether it has descended for 1800 years in a succession of Popes and Bishops, or [was] brought down from Heaven by the holy Ghost in the form of a Dove, in a Phyal of holy Oil? *

Adams, who had devoted the first of his *Novanglus* letters to a defense of the right of revolution, was uncharacteristically

---

* *The Adams-Jefferson Letters,* ed. Lester J. Cappon, 2 vols. (Chapel Hill, 1959), II, 445. Religious Adams certainly was, but his faith was closer to Deism than to the Calvinism of his Puritan forebears. Rejecting Rousseau's arguments for the natural equality of mankind, he compared them to the "sophistry" of the Athanasian Creed and to the doctrine of transubstantiation. Ibid. p. 355.

ecstatic when opportunity came to frame a new government. "How few of the human race," he wrote in 1776, have ever made a government "for themselves or their children! When, before the present epocha, had three millions of people full power and a fair opportunity to form and establish the wisest and happiest government that human wisdom can contrive?" * He soon had a chance to try his hand at making a government. He became chief architect of the Massachusetts Constitution of 1780, the preamble of which is modeled on Locke: "The body politic is formed by a voluntary association of individuals. It is a social compact. . . ." The right of revolution is written into the preamble. The first article, based on the Declaration of Independence, asserts, in Adams's draft, that "All men are born equally free and independent, and have certain natural, essential, and unalienable rights. . . ." [30] Proudly, Adams asserted that he had reduced Locke, Sidney, Rousseau, and Mably to a practicable scheme.[31] The claim does not sound like a repudiation of these thinkers.

Against European critics, Adams wrote in 1787 his famous *Defense of the Constitutions of Government,* in which he praised the establishment of the American states as "a great point gained in favor of the rights of mankind." [32] Of those who formed the governments of the states, he commented: "It will never be pretended that [they] had interviews with the gods, or were in any degree under the inspiration of Heaven. . . . It will forever be acknowledged that these governments were contrived . . . by reason and the senses." [33] The Convention at Philadelphia he looked forward to as "the greatest single effort of national deliberation that the world has ever seen." [34] Three years later, when Richard Price sent him the sermon which had occasioned

---

* *Works,* IV, 200. Sending a circular letter to the state governors in 1783, George Washington exhibited the same enthusiasm: "The foundation of our Empire was not laid in the gloomy age of Ignorance and Superstition, but at an Epocha when the rights of mankind were better understood and more clearly defined, than at any former period. . . ." *Writings,* ed. J. C. Fitzpatrick, 39 vols. (Washington, D.C., 1931–44), XXVI, 485.

Burke's furious reflections, Adams replied that "the whole scope of my life has been to support such principles and propagate such sentiments." [35]

Like Washington, who greeted the initiation of the French Revolution with questions about the future course of events, Adams expressed a good deal of skepticism in 1790 and came, in time, to share Burke's disgust with the Reign of Terror that followed the hopeful days of 1789.[36] But Adams condemned the Jacobins from within the framework of their assumptions. His son published a series of letters in the *Columbian Centinel* (1791) under the name of *Publicola*. In these letters, which many assumed on the basis of style and sentiment to have come from Adams himself, John Quincy Adams condemned the excesses of the French Revolution, and specifically dissociated himself from the criticisms made by Burke. In this, he was true to his father, who had scribbled disagreements into the margins of his four copies of Rousseau's *Contrat Social* ("Mad rant") but was forced nonetheless to pay tribute to Rousseau's positive points: "The speculative genius and unequalled eloquence of this writer has pulled down systems; it has invalidated errors; it has undermined impostures; but it has not discovered truth. It remains for others to erect new systems which may be better or may be worse." [37] The implicit call for "new systems" was not derived from Burke or from any other believer in prescription.

Objecting to Condorcet, Adams wrote against the means rather than the ends of the *philosophes*:

> The public mind was improving in knowledge and the public heart in humanity, equity, and benevolence; the fragments of feudality, the inquisition, the rack, the cruelty of punishments, Negro slavery were giving way. . . . But the philosophers must arrive at perfection per saltum.[38]

Using metaphors of artifice rather than of nature, he scorned the "Gilding and false Lustre" of hereditary nobility, whom Burke admired as "great oaks" above the vegetable commons.[39] He agreed with Jefferson that a natural aristocracy existed in every society. Birth and wealth give advantages to some as talent and virtue aid others.[40] But the *Discourses on Davila*, published in the same year as Burke's *Reflections*, posit an indispensable upper house in every legislature in order to box in the aristocracy, to prevent them from complete domination of the government.[41] In the margin of Mary Wollstonecraft's history of the French Revolution, Adams scrawled, "Arm a power above [aristocracy] and another below it; or if you will, one on its right hand, the other on its left: both able to say to it, when it grows mad, 'Maniac! keep within your limits.' "[42]

There is no doubt that Adams wanted government to be characterized by deference, ceremony, and even ritual. William Maclay and other egalitarians in the first Congress found much in "His Rotundity" to outrage them. But Adams advocated formality as a dike against the flood of democracy. He was himself no monarchist and no aristocrat in the traditional sense. He feared tyranny in a thousand forms, and had no faith whatsoever in that great Conservative illusion, a class of men fit to rule other men. Working out checks and counterchecks, he was, like the Madison of *Federalist No. 10,* a pessimistic Liberal.

Adams recognized, as Burke did not, the evils of the *ancien régime*. He understood, as Burke did not, the philosophical basis of the Enlightenment's criticism of traditional society. He knew what it was that the prophets of progress hoped to achieve. What he did not understand, for all his condemnations of it, was the entrenched power of the First and Second Estates. He imagined naïvely that the Jacobins could have dealt with Louis XVI and with the Roman Catholic Church as the rebels of America had dealt with George III and the Anglican clergy. It was not that easy. Geographically and historically, the obstacles to the French Revolution were present in a way that Americans could scarcely imagine. "The paradox," writes Edward Handler, "is that elaborate in his resort to history [as he was], Adams was yet quite unhistorical. Reducing the variety of history to a rigid pattern, he stressed uniformity and constancy, rather than change, in the treatment of his data." [43] Randall Ripley, in an essay that underlines the differences between Adams and Burke, agrees. Adams viewed the French Revolution as most Americans have viewed revolutions abroad, with the rationalistic and ahistorical assumptions of Liberalism. [44]

Closer to Conservatism than most of the Federalists, he remained "a *philosophe* in spite of himself." [45] No wonder then his most satisfactory correspondent, once the heat of party battle had cooled, was Thomas Jefferson. No wonder he confided to him, in a letter about the French Revolution, that the eighteenth century was, despite its errors and follies, "the most honourable to human Nature." [46] His last words were these: "Thomas Jefferson survives." His concern was for the future and not for the past.

Alexander Hamilton, whom Adams reviled as a bastard brat of a Scotch peddler, is another story. He, too, has been called a Conservative in the line of Burke. He, too, as a young man, spoke of "the natural rights of mankind" and of the "rational faculties" by which man discovers natural law. His *Full Vindication of the Measures of the Congress* was fired off in 1774 in reply to Samuel Seabury's *Westchester Farmer* pamphlets. When Seabury answered that New York had no charter rights because it had no charter, Hamilton shot back like a *philosophe:* "The sacred rights of mankind are not to be rummaged for among old parchments or musty records. They are written, as with a sunbeam, in the whole volume of human nature, by the hand of the Divinity itself, and can never be erased or obscured by mortal power." [47]

But he was not always so sanguine about human nature nor so sunny about the right of revolution. He came into his own in the struggle over ratification of the Constitution and in the first years of Washington's Administration. The Framers had rejected his authoritarian proposals for an executive who would be, in effect, an elected monarch and for a Senate that would serve for life, but his position as Washington's factotum gave him all the chance he needed to tighten the bonds of nationhood and to make the powerful more powerful still. He was probably sincere when he assured Edward Carrington, in 1792, that he was "affectionately attached to the republican theory," [48] but he was no friend of liberty in his militancy at the time of the Whisky Rebellion and in his enthusiasm for the Alien and Sedition Laws. His most agile apologists confess that his plans to subvert the election of 1800 were a blot on his record, and his detractors have found good reason to charge him with disloyalty to Washington during the negotiations that led to Jay's Treaty of 1795. [49] If "Right" and "Left" refer to sympathy for and allegiance to the top and the bottom of the socio-economic scale, Hamilton was definitely what Rossiter calls him, a "man of the Right" rather than a Conservative.

He was most Liberal in his ready application of human reason to the problems of social innovation. Confronted by the perilous state of public credit, he created a funding system and a national bank to stablize the economy. Presented with the economic advantages of an industrial over an agricultural society, he attempted to use the power of the government to advance manufacturers. He opted for the new, for industrial capitalism, and helped to undermine the agrarian order upon which Conservative society has always rested.

He was least Liberal in his love of power. Henry Adams, who inherited his great-grandfather's loathing for Hamilton, is responsible for the continued currency of the counterfeit anecdote in which Hamilton is said to have called the people a "Great Beast." [50] Hamilton probably did say something like this more than once, but another anecdote better distinguishes him from his contemporaries (few of whom were really fond of the "inferior sort" of society). Looking once at Jefferson's portraits of Francis Bacon, Isaac Newton, and John Locke, Hamilton asked his host who they were and learned that Jefferson thought them the three greatest men the world had ever produced. Hamilton, after a moment's thought, retorted, "The greatest man that ever lived

. . . was Julius Caesar." [51] Like the Roman dictator, Hamilton was ready to overturn established institutions and to rule without the legitimacy conferred by tradition. Thomas Hutchinson's judgment of Governor Dudley serves for Hamilton as well: "I think it is no more than justice to his character, to allow that he had as many virtues as can consist with so great a thirst for honor and power." [52]

At the time when Hamilton, Madison, and Jay were setting forth the *rationale* of the Constitution, Jonathan Jackson published a short book entitled *Thoughts upon the Political Situation*. Jackson was a member of the notorious "Essex Junto," a group that played a Conservative role in Massachusetts politics. His book is useful to historians because he helps to place Adams and Hamilton in the spectrum of post-revolutionary political thought. Jackson found the proposed Constitution too Liberal. The danger in the United States was from an excess of democracy. (Jackson lived within a day's ride of the scene of Shays's Rebellion.) There was no real problem with aristocracy: "I had rather have wise men govern me, even though at times they should be severe, than fools. . . . Mankind are abundantly happier, when obliged to conform strictly to rules, if they are wise ones; as the children of the same family are, to those of a well regulated house, than where each one may do as he pleases. . . ." [53] As the metaphor suggests, Jackson preferred paternalism.

By an indirect election so complicated that the Electoral College seems anarchic by comparison, Jackson hoped to secure a "steady government" to restrain the people. He suggested a model of administrative hierarchy—the Chinese bureaucracy. He approved of a rigorous militia system to indoctrinate the population in the virtues of subordination. "Who can govern properly in any department that has not learned to obey?" [54] Eventually, Jackson had to accept the Constitution as the best that could be had.

Associated with him in the Essex Junto was Fisher Ames, who played an important role in the first four Congresses (1789–97).

Although not a royalist,[55] Ames lamented the vogue of Locke and Paine and condemned the notion that "all the citizens of a republic have an equal right to political power." [56] Like Jonathan Boucher, he conceived of liberty as the product of restraint: "Liberty is not to be enjoyed, indeed it cannot exist, without the habits of just subordination; it consists, not so much in removing all restraint from the orderly, as in imposing it on the violent." [57] He was, as a lawyer, actively involved in the enforcement of the Sedition Acts. Like Increase and Cotton Mather, he held fast to old-fashioned doctrines. Vernon Parrington flogged Ames with the ferocity that New England malefactors always roused in him, but even the most compassionate modern account of his career ends with an admission, "He misjudged the direction and import of the American democratic movement." [58] In his own life, Ames recognized that the Federalists had lost ground in the struggle with the Jeffersonians. Retreating to journalism, he found the *New England Palladium* in 1801, but the essays he published there and in the *Boston Repertory* and the *Monthly Anthology* are melancholy commentaries on disaster rather than calls to renew the battle.[59]

Conservative the Essex Junto was; politically influential it was not. "The Essexmen," writes David Hackett Fischer, "were Conservative in the double sense that they resisted change and sought to restrict the power of the people; their Conservatism was ideological, for they defended not merely a fixed position but fixed principles." [60] In the excellent essay from which this quotation comes, Fischer shows that the Essex Junto was never the force in Massachusetts politics that John Adams thought it was. Twelve men are usually placed in the group: Fisher Ames, George Cabot, Francis Dana, Nathan Dane, Benjamin Goodhue, Stephen Higginson, Jonathan Jackson, John Lowell, Theophilus Parsons, Timothy Pickering, Israel Thorndike, and Nathaniel Tracy. Of them, only Pickering and Thorndike were politically active after 1797. Their Conservatism was the cause of their rapid decline from positions of influence even within the Federalist party of their native state. David Hackett Fischer's book, *The Revolution of American Conservatism,* is a social-scientific corroboration of the main point of Dixon Ryan Fox's classic study of the decline of aristocracy in New York: the new nation had no place for an authentically Conservative political party.

It is undeniable that the merchants and lawyers who formed the middle-class elite of Federalist New England continued to receive deference long after their political power was gone. The Brahmins of Beacon Hill had social status in nineteenth-century America, and they still enjoy, in some circles, considerable prestige. Sociological studies like E. Digby Baltzell's *Philadelphia Gentlemen* and *The Protestant Establishment* indicate that certain businesses and professions are *still* dominated by the old families. But status in American society does not last indefinitely without political and economic power won in competition with new men forever "on the make."

Fischer's analysis, which challenges earlier theories of the discouragement of the Federalists after 1800,[61] indicates that the younger generation of Federalists used Timothy Pickering and other surviving Essexmen as ceremonial props while they, the young activists, "came to terms with every major argument of the Jeffersonians—majoritarianism, individuality, the ever-broadening concept of equality, states' rights, even agrarianism and Anglophobia." [62] They tried whatever seemed to work—multilevel party organization, newspapers, barbecues, rallies, stump speeches, parades and festivals, "free transportation to the polls, outright bribery, and corruption of all kinds. . . ." [63] In his magisterial *Life and Letters of Harrison Gray Otis,* Samuel Eliot Morison notes that the native aristocracy of Boston "abandoned none of their conservative principles" when they cast their lot with the Revolution.[64] But the limited political success of Harrison Gray Otis, who was senator from Massachusetts, 1817–22, and mayor of Boston, 1829–31, depended upon just such an abandonment of the few tendencies to Conservatism that persisted into the nineteenth century. It was all very well for Rufus King to write to Christopher Gore in 1816, "Federalists of our age must be content with the past," [65] but younger men had their way to make in a society that adored Andrew Jackson as one of its own.

3   The Paradox of Southern Liberalism

The most significant attempt to institutionalize an American version of Conservatism was made by the plantation South in the three decades prior to the Civil War. While Federalists came to accept and Whigs to glorify the age of commercial enterprise, the Southern planter took himself to be a Cavalier, the literal and symbolic descendant of the English gentry who fought for King Charles and toasted Prince Charlie. Although the romances of Sir Walter Scott had their vogue above the Mason-Dixon line, Northerners never took the Waverly Novels as seriously as Southerners did. While Northerners toiled in offices and mills, the Southern elite staged tournaments with trumpets, heraldic devices, and fully armored knights.* While the Lowells built factories, the Lees and the Randolphs remained loyal to the land. This, at least, was the picture painted by the South.

The crucial question is this: Was the institutional basis of Southern society fundamentally Conservative or Liberal? If the former, then the cult of chivalry was the derivative of an integrated social system. If the latter, it was—from a sympathetic point of view—a brave affirmation of the ideal in the face of the actual. From an unsympathetic point of view, the ostentatious medievalism of the South was mere flummery, an exercise in "false consciousness," an attempt to make of whole cloth a lifestyle not found in the fabric of Southern society.

Southerners proclaimed, and still proclaim, that kinship is more important to them than to Northerners. There was, indeed, a difference in the Southern conception of the family. A handful

* For a description of a Southern tournament, see Rollin G. Osterweis, *Romanticism and Nationalism in the Old South* (New Haven, 1949), pp. 3–5. Mark Twain, who deplored the influence of Scott, was sure that Scott had all but caused the Civil War. See Chapter 46 of *Life on the Mississippi*.

of families in Virginia and South Carolina *had* achieved a socially superior position acknowledged by all, however reluctantly. Marked deference *was* paid to the men who owned hundreds of slaves and lived in Greek Revival mansions. The sense of kinship *did* extend further than in the North. The position of women, at least of planters' wives, *was* elevated above that of Northern females.

But most of the differences between North and South were minor compared to the cultural norms shared by both sections. The status of the "First Families of Virginia," like that of the descendants of the first colonists of Massachusetts Bay, was declining. Deference was paid, North and South, to wealth: "The 'aristocracy' included owners of large plantations with many slaves as well as some of the wealthy urban 'factors' and merchants and those in the learned professions. . . . The upper middle class included small planters, commercial farmers, lesser merchants and professionals." [66] New money meant status little below that of old money. Respect was given to new money in preference to impoverished gentility.

The apotheosis of woman was a phenomenon of middle-class culture, an aspect of Victorianism rather than a vestige of knightly times; it was certainly not a survival from the Conservative world of eighteenth-century Europe. The concept of the family common to North and South was middle-class rather than aristocratic. In technical terms, the family was conjugal or nuclear rather than extended. It was "neolocal" (i.e. independently located) rather than patrilocal or matrilocal. The nuclear family of father, mother, and children served as "the effective residence, consumption, and social unit." *

* The quoted phrase is taken from Robin M. Williams, Jr., *American Society: A Sociological Interpretation* (rev. ed., New York, 1960), p. 51. Williams's entire discussion of the American family is excellent; see pp. 39–85. Another valuable account is Talcott Parsons, *Essays in Sociological Theory* (rev. ed., Glencoe, Ill., 1954), pp. 177–96. A brilliant account of the development of the middle-class family that we take, wrongly, to be typical of society before the eighteenth century is Philippe Ariès, *Centuries of Childhood* (London, 1962).

The American family, Northern and Southern, was, even in the nineteenth century, characterized by a high degree of equality in the relation of paternal and maternal in-laws to the conjugal family, in the relation of husband to wife (compared to the authority of the European husband), in the relation of parents to children (compared, again, to European customs), and in the relation of siblings to each other. The Southern family was definitely not aristocratic by European standards. Conservative societies are based on quite different conceptions of kinship. The aristocratic family is extended vertically rather than horizontally; it is a "line" of fathers and sons the continuity and status of which is socially recognized and legally enhanced by primogeniture, entail, and the subordination of interests interfering with patrilineal succession. Southern families who approximated Conservatism in kinship system and domestic relations were atypical even in the heyday of the Cotton Kingdom. The sons and daughters of a deceased "cavalier" were likely to sell the depleted land, divide the proceeds, the slaves, and the miscellaneous assets, and set out in various directions to form independent households related chiefly by memory and united only on the most ceremonial occasions. The Southern family was admirably integrated into the highly rationalized economic and political system of a Liberal society.

The economy of the South, unlike the Southern family, has been the subject of intensive research and scholarly debate. The myth of the Conservative South receives remarkable support in Eugene D. Genovese's closely reasoned Marxist analysis, *The Political Economy of Slavery*. Genovese argues that the South was not capitalist in its agriculture, that slavery and the master-slave relationship made the South a "premodern" enclave in a predominantly bourgeois nation.

> If for a moment we accept the designation of the planters as capitalists and of the slave system as a form of capitalism, we are then confronted by a capitalist society that impeded the development of every normal feature of capitalism. The planters

were not mere capitalists; they were precapitalists, quasi-aristocratic landowners who had to adjust their economy and ways of thinking to a capitalist world market. Their society, in its spirit and fundamental direction, represented the antithesis of capitalism, however many compromises it had to make.[67]

Although Genovese shows brilliantly why the South could not industrialize under the slave system, his argument about the nature of Southern society depends upon definitions which emphasize industrialism to the exclusion of agrarian capitalism. The truth of the matter is that Southern planters invested in lands with an eye to profit, produced staple crops for sale on the world market, and understood international trade well enough to threaten nullification when Northern manufacturers forced into law a protective tariff, in 1828, that was clearly disadvantageous to the Southern economy.

Noting that the South provided 80 per cent of England's imported cotton, Barrington Moore, Jr., insists that slavery "was no anachronistic excrescence on industrial capitalism. It was an integral part of this system and one of its prime motors in the world at large." Moore goes on to underline his point: "The supposed aristocratic and precommercial or anticommercial virtues of the plantation aristocracy rested on the strictly commercial profits of slavery." [68] Although many planters treated their slaves with kindness, the essential fact is that the Negro slave was defined in the legal codes as a species of property rather than as a man. Slaves were bought and sold and bred. Frederick Law Olmsted's *The Cotton Kingdom* is a storehouse of references to the South's concern for the monetary rather than the human value of the slave. The metaphor of the plantation as an extended family seems absurd when placed next to newspaper columns commiserating with owners whose valuable property has drowned or, alas, run away.

Harriet Beecher Stowe, frequently maligned by those who have never read her, goes to the heart of the matter when she dramatizes the plight of a slave-owner, a devout Christian, who must sell the slaves that he really does love. When his wife asks him why he selected his favorites rather than others for whom he had less affection, his answer rings out as an indictment of the entire system: "Because they will bring the highest sum of any, that's why."

Stanley Elkins has theorized that the "dynamics of unopposed capitalism" made slavery in the United States more stark, more terrible, than in Latin America.[69] Scholars who have disagreed with Elkins have disputed his statements about Latin America, which was more capitalistic than Elkins allowed; they have suggested that racial rather than economic attitudes account for the difference between the two systems; but they have not questioned the basic assumption that Southern planters sought profit as avidly as did Northern manufacturers.[70]

What is true of the South's economy is equally true of its politics. With the exception of the Negro, who was by racist definition outside the boundary of Southern citizenship, the South was as much a part of Jacksonian democracy as the North. The South moved, as the North did, toward universal white manhood suffrage, the abolition of property qualifications for voters and for officeholders, the popular election of all officers, the periodic reapportionment of representation on the basis of population rather than wealth, and a society characterized by a high degree of social mobility.[71] If wide participation in public affairs and diffusion of leadership are elements in a democratic system, then the Southern frontier was very nearly as democratic as the Northern frontier.[72] Although Virginia and South Carolina were less egalitarian than Alabama and Mississippi, six of the last eight governors of prewar Virginia rose from the yeomanry.[73] It was a rough-and-tumble world, from which the affluent few took time out, infrequently, to stage a tournament.

In the realm of political theory, the South was—except on the question of race—more Liberal than the North. John Randolph of Roanoke and John Taylor of Caroline carried on the tradition of Jefferson rather than that of Burke. Russell Kirk, in his biography of Randolph, has turned him upside down and shaken from his pockets every shred of evidence that links him to English Conservatism, but even Kirk admits that the eccentric Virginian did "not share Burke's admiration for the party system and lacked Burke's veneration of the State" and was, in his attitude toward political power, imbued with "the Jeffersonian 'necessary evil' spirit."[74] Most historians have preferred to follow Henry Adams, who characterized Randolph (in a letter) as a "lunatic monkey" and (in a biography) as an erratic formulator of dogmatic Liberalism.[75]

Randolph, Taylor, and the other "Old Republicans" recently studied by Norman K. Risjord were the "heirs not of Edmund Burke but of the *philosophes* and the Enlightenment."[76] Randolph came to prominence in the protracted conflict over the Yazoo lands. Despite the protests of Randolph and the other "Old Republicans," John Marshall handed down a decision in *Fletcher* v. *Peck* (1810) that upheld the Federalist faith in the sanctity of contract against the argument that the majority in Georgia had the right to overturn and undo a fraudulently made contract for the sale of land. Judge Spencer Roane of Virginia, an ally of Randolph and Taylor, was Jefferson's nomination for Chief Justice and John Marshall's most bitter judicial foe. One cannot have it both ways. If Russell Kirk chooses to lament the influence of the "doctrinaire" sage of Monticello, he cannot logically praise the same doctrines when held by John Randolph and John Taylor of Caroline.

The Old Republicans were a minority group within the Monroe faction that was itself a minority within the Democratic party (dominated by Madison), but John C. Calhoun is a different matter. The "Iron Man" from South Carolina was, of course, conservative in the relative sense of the term—he was anxious to keep intact the institutions of Southern society. But his conservatism was in the form of dedication to and trust in Liberal institutions. His long campaign on behalf of states' rights employed the doctrine of Nullification, derived from the Virginia and Kentucky Resolutions which Madison and Jefferson had aimed against the Alien and Sedition Laws. Calhoun feared power (because he saw it increase in the hands of men unconvinced of the necessity of slavery) and proclaimed his faith in liberty. As the crisis of Nullification came on, Calhoun wrote to Andrew Jackson (June 4, 1826): "An issue has been fairly made between *power* and *liberty;* and it must be determined in the next three years, whether the real governing principle in our political system be the power and patronage of the Executive, or the voice of the people." [77] His famous rebuke to Jackson, in the form of a toast at the Jefferson Day Dinner of 1830, was in the spirit of the man honored by the occasion: "The Union—next to our liberty most dear." [78]

Defeated in the struggle over Nullification, Calhoun turned, like a classic Liberal, to the checks-and-balances of a written Constitution. The *Disquisition on Government* (1851) denies the Liberal theory of the social compact by which man moved from a state of nature to a state of civil government: "In no age or country has any society or community ever been found, whether enlightened or savage, without government of some description." [79] But Calhoun's scornful rejection of the social-compact theory of the origin of government does not preclude his adoption of the Liberal theory of the purpose of government. He describes government functionally and insists on the "right on the part of the ruled to choose their rulers at proper intervals and to hold them thereby responsible for their conduct" because "the responsibility of the rulers to the ruled, through the right of suffrage, is the indispensable and primary principle in the *foundation* of a constitutional government." [80] The use of "foundation" (the emphasis is Calhoun's) is itself indicative of the social-compact theory which was rejected half-a-dozen pages earlier.

In typically Liberal fashion, Calhoun defines "constitution" as whatever prevents the abuse of power, and sets as the practical problem of the *Disquisition* the tendency of governments to move beyond their negative functions (creation of order) to tyrannical abuse (e.g. the Force Act of 1833). The problem is perennial. "The powers which it is necessary for government to possess in order to repress violence and preserve order cannot execute themselves." They must, therefore, be administered by fallible men whose motives cannot be wholly pure. "And hence the powers vested in them to prevent injustice and oppression on the part of others will, if left unguarded, be by them converted into instruments to oppress the rest of the community." [81] Madison had, in *The Federalist No. 51,* grappled with the same problem: "In framing a government which is to be administered by men over men, the great difficulty lies in this: you must first enable the government to control the governed; and in the next place oblige it to control itself." Madison went on to argue that American society was "broken into so many parts, interests and classes of citizens, that the rights of individuals, or of the minority, will be in little danger from interested combinations of the majority." Calhoun, conscious of the South as a permanent minority against which interests and classes of citizens did combine, proposed a constitutional check to prevent actions injurious to the South.

His proposal was for an "organism" to limit and restrict the powers of government to an essential minimum. The term "organism" is a favorite of Conservatism, but the institution it refers to is manifestly mechanistic. It is, of course, the cumbersome "concurrent majority" by which Calhoun proposed to protect the minority's interests. There was only "one certain mode" by which oppression could be averted, "and that is by taking the sense of each interest or portion of the community . . . separately . . . and to require the consent of each interest either to put or to keep the government in action." [82] In other words, each interest group is to have its veto. As his biographer admits, Calhoun remained at heart a metaphysician rather than a practitioner of politics,[83] and nothing shows it more than his *Disquisition.* The constitution he "fabricated" was an attempt to institutionalize the interest-group politics of a democratic society, to publicize and rationalize much that goes on in the lobbies of Congress. It was an extreme version of the "mixed" government that John Adams proposed, for Adams had contented himself with three social classes while Calhoun wanted to provide for a myriad of interests.

The same conclusion applies to the secession of the Confederate states. If one ignores for a moment the motives behind secession, one sees that the South was more Liberal than the North, for it demanded the right of revolution as the last resort of those who felt that the purposes of the original compact had been subverted. John L. O'Sullivan, erstwhile editor of *The Democratic Review,* was not the only Northerner to feel, in 1863, that the North's effort to prevent secession acted "to stultify our revolution; to blaspheme our very Declaration of Independence; to repudiate all our history. . . ." [84]

Once the Southerners had declared their determination to break the bonds that tied them to what they deemed an alien authority, they wrote themselves a Constitution that was modeled closely, even slavishly, on the Federal Constitution—Bill of Rights and all.[85] In practice, Southern society was often authoritarian and elitist, but when was a political theory ever a sufficient guide to the actions of men? * The paradoxical conclusion, which Louis Hartz makes much of, is that the constitutional theory of the South was an extreme form of Liberalism invented by desperate men determined to preserve the most repressive institution ever devised on this continent—the brutal and brutalizing enslavement of other men.[86]

Randolph and Calhoun were not, of course, the only representatives of Southern polity. There was also the strange, fascinating figure of George Fitzhugh. "The distance between Fitzhugh and Jefferson," writes C. Vann Woodward, "renders the conventional polarities between Jefferson and Hamilton, Jackson and Clay, or

---

* If the military history of the Civil War is any indication, the South was more egalitarian than the North—at least its armies were far less disciplined than those of the Union (which were not disciplined at all by modern standards). See David Donald, "The Sourtherner As A Fighting Man," in Charles Grier Sellers, Jr., *The Southerner as American* (Chapel Hill, 1960), pp. 72–88.

Hoover and Roosevelt—all Liberals under the skin—insignificant indeed. When compared with Fitzhugh, even John Taylor of Caroline, John Randolph of Roanoke, and John C. Calhoun blend inconspicuously into the great American consensus, since they were all apostles in some degree of John Locke." [87] Fitzhugh, who does not appear in Kirk's *Conservative Mind,* went back, like Jonathan Boucher before him, to the work of Sir Robert Filmer. In Filmer's *Patriarcha* Fitzhugh found the theory of the authoritarian, patriarchal family, the model for the plantation and for civil society itself. The metaphor of master-as-father was half the story. With further support from Aristotle and from Carlyle, Fitzhugh set about to demolish the doctrines of Liberalism.

John Locke was the enemy. The Declaration of Independence and the Virginia Bill of Rights were samples of his evil handiwork. "The abstract principles which they enunciate, we candidly admit, are wholly at war with slavery; we shall attempt to show that they are equally at war with all government, all subordination, all order." [88] The Liberal faith in natural rights led directly to a free society, and that was the whole trouble. Free society was without community, without charity. It was a laissez-faire jungle where no man felt responsible for any other man. Fitzhugh looked at the consequences of Liberalism and judged them to be ill. *Cannibals All!* was the telling title of one of his books. And nothing seemed to please him more than his claim that he and Karl Marx, both socialists, were one in their repudiation of capitalism. "Socialism, in some form or another, is universal in free society [as a form of protest against intolerable conditions], and its single aim is to attain the protective influence of slavery." [89] The South, happy in its plantations, already enjoyed the "socialist" society which European thinkers sought in their flight from freedom.

While other Southerners rushed in the direction of equalitarianism (for whites only), Fitzhugh maintained that inequality was right and proper. Slavery was but a hesitant step in the direction of hierarchy.

We agree with Mr. Jefferson that all men have natural and inalienable rights. To violate or disregard such rights, is to oppose the designs and plans of Providence. . . . The order and subordination observable in the physical, animal, and human world show that some are formed for higher, others for lower stations—the few to command, the many to obey. We conclude that about nineteen out of every twenty individuals have "a natural and inalienable right" to be taken care of and protected, to have guardians, trustees, husbands, or masters; in other words, they have a natural and inalienable right to be slaves. The one in twenty are as clearly born or educated or some way fitted for command and liberty. Not to make them rulers or masters is as great a violation of natural right as not to make slaves of the mass.[90]

These archly Conservative opinions were probably shared by many Southerners as they looked out across their cotton fields and watched the slave-gangs at work, as they considered the "poor whites" and their inability to appreciate the classics or even to feed and clothe their families, but few Southerners were bold enough to utter such sentiments in public.

Fitzhugh could afford to be brash; his influence on Southern politics was nil. As Charles Grier Sellers, Jr., remarks, "Southern planters were too much bourgeois capitalists and southern farmers were too much Jacksonian democrats to entertain the neo-feudalists' vituperation at 'free society.' "[91] Fitzhugh's books are literary in the sense that they are projections of values in the form of fantasy. Paradoxically, the literature of the prewar South rivaled Fitzhugh's sociology neither in imaginative power nor in commitment to Conservatism.*

Literature is, as Aristotle pointed out in the *Poetics,* concerned more with probabilities than with possibilities, more with the

---

* Edgar Allan Poe's imaginative power was, of course, considerable, but the whole question of the relation of his work to the South is difficult. One thing does seem fairly clear: he was far too alienated from society to be classified politically as a Conservative. Unlike Fitzhugh, Poe had no conception of what a Conservative society might be like.

ideal than with the actual. Literature is intentionally fictive. Although the novelist is almost by definition concerned with man in society,[92] he is much more free than the social scientist in that his imagined model of human behavior is neither true nor false in any scientific sense. Literature is also, except when completely formalist (i.e. totally involved in its own techniques), concerned with norms and values, for it is, after all, an intentionally emotive use of language. The social scientist describes and predicts, but the novelist is always explicitly or implicitly engaged and committed. Émile Zola, who proclaimed the ideal of objectivity in *Le Roman expérimental* and in his Rougon-Macquart series, was more polemical in his novels than many an unabashed propagandist. Given the nature of literature, one assumes that the major Southern writers went beyond the sociological facts in order to affirm in their art a culture more Conservative than the "real" South that lay about them. But they did not.

With the exception of versified tracts struck off in defense of the "peculiar institution," Southern literature tended to the egalitarianism of frontier humor, or to ambivalent tales in which the Tidewater "aristocrats" receive only qualified support.*

John Pendleton Kennedy, for example, was among the earliest and best known of the writers who made the plantation the scene of their fiction. *Swallow Barn* (1832), an account of the life of Frank and Lucretia Meriwether, is interesting today mainly because of its ambivalence. The Meriwether mansion is described with irony: "Swallow Barn is an aristocratical old edifice which sits, like a brooding hen, on the southern bank of the James River. . . . The main building is more than a century old. It is built with thick brick walls, but one story in height, and surmounted by a double-faced or hipped roof, which gives the idea of a ship

---

* Osterweis, who attempts to make a case for a separate Southern culture in *Romanticism and Nationalism in the Old South,* relies at crucial moments on a handful of poems, especially Henry Timrod's "Ethnogenesis." Although the South had poems praising ancient days and local customs, no Southern poet of this period developed anything coherent or comprehensive enough to be called a Conservative vision of society.

bottom upwards." The brooding hen and the ship's bottom hint
that the mansion is something less than awesome. Frank Meriwether is treated with the same affectionate skepticism. He is, for
instance, High-Church Anglican, but quite ignorant of the doctrines of Christianity. He refers to the *droit du seigneur,* but takes
the phrase to mean the "correctness" of the lord. His cousin, Ned
Hazard, courts a young lady who resembles Don Quixote in the
absurdity of her romantic whims. Kennedy uses her to satirize
the Southern view of womanhood, which was, of course, an exaggerated form of the Victorian worship of the "fairer sex." It is
very difficult to disagree with the assessment of William R. Taylor, perhaps the most perceptive student of the Old South in
American literature: "In most episodes of the book Kennedy
plays with the comic inappropriateness of the chivalric image." [93]

Horse-Shoe Robinson (1835) is Kennedy's second variation on
the idea of chivalry. The hero is not, as Edgar Allan Poe rightly
noted in a review, the South Carolina planter alongside whom the
Scotch-Irish blacksmith fights during the American Revolution.
Despite his lowly origins, his ignoble (by European standards)
trade, and his dialect, Horse-Shoe Robinson proves himself to be
a self-made cavalier. He is one of the first of the endless *levée* of
nature's noblemen.

Two years after the publication of *Swallow Barn,* William
Alexander Caruthers dramatized Bacon's Rebellion in *The Cavaliers of Virginia,* a romance which sets the effete and dissolute
aristocrats of Governor Berkeley's entourage against the fanati-
cally self-righteous veterans of Cromwell's army (who rebel because the government will not protect them from Indian raids).
The novel, which plays fast and loose with the historical facts of
the 1676 uprising, affirms the character of Nathaniel Bacon, who
is neither Cavalier nor Roundhead. Similar is John Esten Cooke's
The Virginia Comedians (1854), a book in which a rouged and
pampered aristocrat, home from abroad, loses the girl to a simple
fisherman named, appropriately, Charles Waters. "The book,"

wrote Cooke himself, "is profoundly democratic, and American—
the aristocracy whom I don't like, [get] the worst of it." [94] Except for the fact that they set their novels in the past (which they
did not see as prescriptive), there is little in Caruthers or Cooke
that can be termed Conservative.

William Gilmore Simms, the most important of the prewar
Southern novelists, is a more complex case because, midway in
his career, he began self-consciously to defend his region against
criticism from the North. He had been, until the 1840's, a literary
nationalist, a member of the "Young America" group (of whom
Evert Duyckinck was the leader), a believer in the mission of
America and in the role of literature in that national mission. [95]
After 1847, when Lorenzo Sabine's *The American Loyalist*
seemed to impugn South Carolina's role in the American Revolution, Simms became a literary sectionalist, perhaps even a Conservative.

Woodcraft (1854), which most critics take to be Simms's best
late work, begins with an aristocratic widow's imperious recovery
of her slaves, and her neighbor's, from a British officer who has
stolen them. But Mrs. Eveleigh, the widow, soon ceases to be the
center of attention. The focus shifts to Mr. Fordham, her overseer,
whose skill in backwoods combat astonishes Mrs. Eveleigh's youthful son. The real hero of the book is, however, Captain Porgy,
a Falstaffian veteran of the wars who enters the novel shouting
for food, drink, and other forms of sensual indulgence. Captain
Porgy is clearly opposed to utilitarian values (symbolized by Mill-
house, his overseer), but he does manage, mostly by luck, to retain
ownership of his ramshackle plantation. The trouble with Porgy
as a heroic representative of Southern values is that he is clownish,
comic, almost porcine. Falstaff without Prince Hal is only half
the play; Liberalism is laughed off the stage, and then the stage
is empty. *Woodcraft,* given its author's ability and ambition,
seems forced and incomplete.

William Taylor's conclusion is concise and persuasive:

The problem for the South was not that it lived by an entirely different set of values and civic ideals but rather that it was forced either to live with the values of the nation at large or— as a desperate solution—to invent others, others which had even less relevance to the Southern situation.[96]

Since the values of the South were the values of the nation at large, the attempt to justify slavery by the *ad hoc* creation of a Conservative way of life was doomed from the start. There was, in American literature, a sustained challenge to Liberal values, but this challenge came from Northerners, from men who did not have to defend in their fiction an indefensible institution. Although Southern writers of the present century have contributed to the myth of a Conservative, Europe-oriented antebellum South, the ironic truth is that Northern novelists in the nineteenth century did more than their Southern counterparts to keep alive the memory of the lost world of Edmund Burke.

II

Images of Value and a Sense of the Past *

1 *From Bracebridge Hall to the Palazzo Roccanera*

Washington Irving has long been identified as the "arch-Federalist of American literature," [1] but the fact is that Irving's Federalism was always *faute de mieux*. The egalitarianism of Jefferson was fair game for Diedrich Knickerbocker, but Irving's *persona* was also a ruthless hunter of the stolid bourgeoisie of mercantile New Amsterdam. And the bourgeoisie was very much at home within the Federalist party. Hamilton believed in strong government to check the democratic impulses of the people, but Hamilton was, as we have seen, an agent of progress in his economic policies; a leader in the transformation of property into the stocks, bonds, and certificates of the modern corporation; an early prophet of what David Bazelon has called "the paper economy." Hamilton's partisans, among whom the young Irving counted himself, snorted at Jeffersonian intellectual qualities, but they themselves were far closer ideologically to Jefferson than to Edmund Burke and the

---

* Parts of this chapter have been adapted from two previously published essays: "Images of Value and the Sense of the Past," *New England Quarterly*, XXXV (1962), 3–26; "Washington Irving and the Conservative Imagination," *American Literature*, XXXVI (1964), 165–73.

47

tradition of English Conservatism. If Irving lost interest in the quarrels of Hamilton and Jefferson, and he did, it was at least in part because he discovered a society more suitable than any in America, an aristocratic order based on continuity rather than on revolution, on landed property rather than on national banks, funded debts, and capitalistic enterprise.[2]

In England and Scotland Irving found what America lacked even under the Federalist administrations of Washington and Adams—a Conservative society with a sense of the past. With due allowance for a tendency to sentimentalize, with account taken for the distance gained by use of his narrator (Geoffrey Crayon), we see him, in 1819, responding as a true Conservative to the European past: England's "every mouldering stone was a chronicle. I longed . . . to tread . . . in the footsteps of antiquity—to loiter about the ruined castle,—to meditate on the falling tower,—to escape . . . from the common-place realities of the present, and lose myself among the shadowy grandeurs of the past."

If Irving's mood were consistently nostalgic, he might be dismissed as a sentimentalist, but, like James Fenimore Cooper, he responded to more than antiquity and ruin. English society provided also a "perpetual volume of reference, wherein are recorded sound deductions from ages of experience. . . ." Where could one turn for "sound deductions"? In his letters, Irving instanced Windsor Castle and Westminster Abbey as symbols of State and Church, and in Westminster Abbey his awe was appropriately religious: "It seems as if the awful nature of the place presses down upon the soul and hushes the beholder into noiseless reverence." But the obscure young traveler from America had little hope of access to royal or ecclesiastical rulers. Where else might one turn? To the "real" England, to the countryside dominated by the estates of the aristocracy and squirarchy. "The great charm . . . of English scenery is the moral feeling that seems to pervade it. It is associated in the mind with ideas of order, of quiet, of sober well-established principles, of hoary usage and reverend custom." Irving's sense of the countryside as locus of order and tradition is like that of Sir Lewis Namier, the great twentieth-century historian of eighteenth-century England.[3] And it is like Edmund Burke's. In a letter to Will Weddell (January 31, 1792), Burke defined the Whig party as the one "connected with the solid, permanent, long-possessed property of the country; a party which, by a temper derived from that species of property, and affording a security to it; was attached to the ancient usages of the kingdom; a party, therefore, essentially constructed upon a groundplot of stability and independence. . . ."

It is no accident that three of the chapters of *The Sketch-Book* and almost all of *Bracebridge Hall* are set upon the "groundplot" of the solid, permanent, and long-possessed ancestral estate. In his instinctive response to England's appeal, Irving happened on images of value which loom large in the Conservative imagination, images comparable in importance to others which have received far more critical attention.

As Henry Nash Smith and R. W. B. Lewis demonstrate, the dominant myth of nineteenth-century America was the myth of the garden: Americans turned to the virgin land as if it were a vehicle by which they could recover the pristine goodness of Adam and Eve before the Fall.[4] Then, in Leo Marx's phrase, came the machine in the garden. The image of the untouched native landscape—and all that it implied—was countered by the image of the machine—and all that *it* implied. The promise of tranquillity, peace, fertility, and a spontaneous relationship to Nature was countered by the threat of turmoil, aggression, sterility, and the repressions of a technological age. But machine and garden are perhaps too stark a contrast. Conservatism as an ideology is an alternative to the dilemma of primitivism or progress. Architectural metaphors are its cardinal images of value.

Writing to Sir Walter Scott shortly after his famous visit to Abbotsford, Irving revealed in his imagery the sources of his political commitments. Although convinced that republicanism was the "best form of government for my own country, yet I feel my poetical associations vividly aroused by the old institutions of this country, and should feel as sorry to see them injured or subverted as I would be to see Windsor Castle or Westminster Abbey demolished to make way for brick tenements."[5] The metaphors are central. While Major L'Enfant and Benjamin Latrobe laid out and constructed public structures for the new nation, the Old World already gloried in the castles, the churches, the country houses that were the visible symbols of its past and of its determination to resist the world of brick tenement and iron factory. The house, especially, is its visible symbol of tradition, of permanence, of man's mastery of the primary environment of civilization.* The machine is stamped with the imprint of the future. The house contains, in Henry James's phrase, "the sense of the past." And Irving was first to feel this. Never a political theorist, Irving was nonetheless the first American writer successfully to articulate the prodigal's discovery of what Hawthorne came to call "Our Old Home."

Irving's initial essays in the direction of Conservatism antedated his voyage to England. He had, in *Salmagundi,* erected Cockloft Hall as a Tory citadel in egalitarian New York. "As the Cocklofts are remarkable for their attachment to everything that has remained long in the family, they are bigoted toward their old edifice, and . . . would sooner have it crumbled about their ears than abandon it." Bracebridge Hall is modeled after Cockloft Hall as well as Abbotsford, and the values ironically held in democratic New York become worthy of serious consideration when found solidly in place on English soil. When the crochety old Cocklofts condemned the customs of the young Republic, they seemed themselves anachronisms more notable for ill-temper than for insight; when Geoffrey Crayon discovers Bracebridge Hall, he speaks for an Irving ready to acknowledge himself attracted to values and institutions whose antiquity proved their viability. Bracebridge Hall, in Yorkshire, is the scene of the amours of Julia Templeton, a ward of the squire, and Guy Brace-

* Writers in revolt against Conservatism have used houses as visible symbols of what they deplore. For comments on Henry Thoreau and Mark Twain, see Allen Guttmann, "Images of Value and the Sense of the Past," 5–8.

bridge, the squire's second son. The plot is trivial. The narrative interest is most intense when Julia, recovering from a fall, hears the story of "The Student of Salamanca." Fortunately, narrative interest is not the only kind. Before Julia and Guy wed, the reader has been introduced into the intricacies of family ties among the gentry, to the daily routine of life among the upper classes, to horsemanship and hawking—in short, to the orderly world of settled society as Irving found it in England, as Irving attempted to recreate it at Sunnyside, as Cooper hoped to rebuild it at Cooperstown.

But even English society is threatened by disorder. The threat is a double one. The neighborhood is, first, menaced by the arrival of Mr. Faddy, a "substantial manufacturer" who has remodeled an old country seat until "it looks not unlike his own manufactory." Mr. Faddy, like Dickens's Mr. Gradgrind, urges the squire to prohibit the celebration of May Day. When Mr. Faddy departs, the squire, who is "at the bottom of these May-day revels," denounces manufacturers as a class: "What's to become of merry old England, when its manor-houses are all turned into manufactories, and its sturdy peasantry into pin-makers and stocking weavers?" What will happen when England becomes "a region of fire; reeking with coal-pits, and furnaces, and smelting-houses, vomiting forth flames and smoke"? The Industrial Revolution has also brought radical readers of Cobbett, men equally impatient with traditional society *and* with Mr. Faddy's utilitarianism. On Geoffrey Crayon's first visit to the hall, the squire told him the nation had altered. Peasants had "broken asunder from the higher class" and had begun "to read newspapers, listen to alehouse politicians, and talk of reform."

When Geoffrey Crayon returns, the squire's fears have become reality. In the village taproom is an agitator, a newspaper-reader who has shocked the villagers "by talking lightly of the Squire and his family; and hinting that it would be better the park should be cut up into small farms and kitchen-gardens, or feed good mutton instead of worthless deer." Happily, one of the villagers is present to defend the good old ways with "half a dozen maxims, which he advances on all occasions." The lower-class threat is turned aside and the middle-class threat fails to stop the May Day fete, but Irving has nonetheless suggested what Cooper was soon to insist upon: the hierarchical society of the eighteenth century was doomed by democratic revolution. Irving and Cooper lived to see the passage of the Reform Bill and the end of the Corn Laws.

Judged by its plot, *Bracebridge Hall* deserves much of the abuse it has received, but there is more to the book than romance and political implication. The mansion and its grounds are, in Irving's phrase, a "fertile subject for study," and they give the book a solidity like that which Cooper achieved with the same symbol of the ancestral mansion in the novels he devoted to the virtues of a landed aristocracy in control of an established society. Brace-bridge Hall is a country mansion, but those who wish to discern the primitive in the tended groves will be disappointed. Irving could, in a fit of enthusiasm, hymn "the glorious independence of man in a savage state," but his second thoughts led him always to conclude that the "Indian of poetical fiction is, like the shep-herd of pastoral romance, a mere personification of imaginary attributes." [6] The "sacred groves" that stirred his imagination were neither Bryant's sylvan temples nor Natty Bumppo's prairie; his groves surround homes and are valuable not as reservoirs of natural value but as reminders of "the ever-interesting story of human existence." It is their "moral associations" and their rela-tion to history that attract Irving's attention. Alluding to the estate lauded by Ben Jonson in "To Penshurst," Irving asks, "Who can walk, with soul unmoved, among the stately groves . . . where the gallant, the amiable, the elegant Sir Philip Sidney passed his boyhood . . . ?" [7]

Irving was by no means unaware of this relation between politi-cal principle and landed property. The squire asserts that "the boasted imitation of nature in modern gardening [has] sprung up with modern republican notions, but [does] not suit a monarchical government; it smacked of the levelling system . . ." Geoffrey Crayon smiles at this "introduction of politics into gardening," but all the context buttresses the squire's conviction that a stand against change must be taken on a wide front or not at all.

It should be clear from the argument above that Irving's letter to Scott contains architectural metaphors which Irving did not use carelessly. With this in mind, we may respond to Irving's half-comic, half-pathetic, letter to Mrs. John Pendleton Kennedy, written near the end of his life, and reverting to the central metaphor as Irving's imagination undoes the Industrial and the Democratic Revolutions:

> I should like nothing better than to have plenty of money to squander on stone and mortar, and to build chateaux. . . , but I would first blow up all the cotton mills . . . and make picturesque ruins of them; and I would utterly destroy the railroad; and all the cotton lords should live in baronial castles . . . and the cotton spinners should be virtuous peasantry of both sexes. . . .[8]

And his last words were these: "I am getting ready to go; I am shutting up my doors and windows."

The Sketch-Book and *Bracebridge Hall* represent a movement from Federalism to a variety of Burkean Conservatism instinctively rather than rationally held. Irving interests readers today precisely because he could respond both to the necessity for an order and hierarchical society *and* to the vision of the American Adam on the virgin land. Although Irving never moved as far in the direction of primitivism as Cooper did, he too, with less intensity, set the antisocial frontier hero against the institutions of society. *The Sketch-Book* contains "Rip Van Winkle" and "The Legend of Sleepy Hollow" as well as Bracebridge Hall. Significantly, these tales are told by Diedrich Knickerbocker rather than by Geoffrey Crayon, perhaps because the latter had become too closely associated with Europe to speak out very strongly for America.

Irving's sympathy for Rip is clear. Less obvious is his very severe qualification of the world Rip returns to. In place of his friends, Rip finds the politician: "a lean bilious-looking fellow, with his pockets full of handbills, was haranguing vehemently about the rights of citizens—elections—members of congress— liberty—Bunker's Hill—heroes of seventy-six—and other words, which were a perfect Babylonish jargon to the bewildered Van Winkle." Not all the irony is directed against dismayed Rip when he says, "I am a poor quiet man, a native of the place, and a loyal subject of the King, God bless him!" Introduced to his son Rip, the old man is confused by change:

> I'm not myself—I'm somebody else—that's me yonder. . . .
> I was myself last night, but I fell asleep on the mountains, and
> they've changed my gun, and every thing's changed, and I'm
> changed, and I can't tell what's my name, or who I am!

It would be nonsense to claim that Irving felt the American Revolution a change for the worse, yet the tale is a gentle reminder that revolution, as Burke insisted in the *Reflections* disrupts "the unchangeable constancy" of society's "decay, failure, renovation, and progression" through the orderly sequence of generations of men. Moreover, if one accepts Philip Young's account of the tale as an archetype of separation from the world, discovery, and return, it is a cautionary tale about the evasion of responsibility. Rip has avoided "all the obligations of maturity: occupation, domestic and financial responsibility, and political position, duty to society in time of war." [9]

The resolution in "Rip Van Winkle" is, with many reservations, on the side of the new; "The Legend of Sleepy Hollow" is much more clearly and outspokenly a prefiguration of the tradition of Mark Twain and the frontier humorists of the middle nineteenth century. Moving from the English countryside to the American, Irving in the first paragraphs of the story alludes to the "ancient Dutch navigators" of the Tappan Zee, as the Hudson was first known, and to the "original Dutch settlers" of Sleepy Hollow. The peace and plenty of the valley are disturbed by two intruders, one real and one mythical, Ichabod Crane of Connecticut and the ghost of a Hessian trooper. Before the tale is over, the first is repelled by a Dutchman in the guise of the second.

Ichabod Crane and Brom Bones compete for Katrina Van Tassel, whose virtues are those of the settled landscape itself; she is a "blooming lass of fresh eighteen, plump as a partridge; ripe and melting and rosy cheeked as one of her father's peaches. . . ." With her go her father's bounty of troops of porkers, squadrons of geese, fleets of ducks, and regiments of turkeys. The competition is for affluence, the basic flaw in Ichabod's candidacy is his inability to accept God's plenty (and Van Tassel's) for what it is; Ichabod, like the archetypal capitalist, imagines not enjoyment but profit: "his heart yearned after the damsel who was to inherit these domains, and his imagination expanded with the idea, how they might be readily turned into cash, and the money invested in immense tracts of wild land, and shingle palaces in the wilderness."

Gangly, spindle-necked, glassy-eyed, snipe-nosed, book-learned Ichabod fights with the only weapons he has—the arts of civilized life. From his strongholds in school and church he sallies forth quixotically "like a knight-errant in quest of adventures"; leaving his unfinished verses behind, he advances "under cover of his character as a singing-master." The climax of the struggle for Katrina comes when Ichabod, crane-like, dances for the favor of his mistress.

Brom Bones is, of course, everything Ichabod is not. He is the "burly, roaring, roystering" hero of the country round, "which rang with his feats of strength and hardihood." A rider and a fighter, he approaches Katrina with "the gentle caresses and endearments of a bear, yet it was whispered that she did not altogether discourage his hopes." In Daniel Hoffman's slightly exaggerated analysis, he becomes a "Catskill Mike Fink, a Ring-Tailed Roarer from Kinderhook." [10]

Ichabod's wise reluctance to fight with his fists leaves uncouth Brom at a disadvantage. But when Baltus Van Tassel begins to gossip about the past, Brom sees his chance and, as everyone knows, surprises Ichabod on his way home that night, as he passes the tree near which Major André had been captured. Ichabod is startled, as the accomplice of Benedict Arnold had been, and quite literally brought down from his high-horse by a pumpkin-head. The Dutch of Sleepy Hollow have won their comic war for cultural independence. The schoolhouse falls into decay while the erstwhile schoolmaster goes off on a middle-class career as lawyer, judge, and politician. Meanwhile, Brom Bones conducts "the blooming Katrina in triumph to the altar." It was Irving, not Augustus Baldwin Longstreet, Thomas Bangs Thorpe, or Mark Twain, who first hit upon the characteristic pattern of American humor, and Irving, not Cooper, who first demonstrated how hard it was for an American writer to dramatize Conservative values unambiguously.

Reviewing *Bracebridge Hall* in the *Literary and Scientific Repository* for May 1822, Cooper complained that Irving had gone too far in his eulogies of British aristocracy and that the book was an ill-composed medley of materials rather than a finished work of art: "It is a sort of series, or rather a given number, of sketches and descriptions of squires and maids and matrons and bachelors and lovesick girls and schoolmasters and priests and apothecaries and doctors and dogs. . . ." [11] Cooper had written his first novel because of the incompetence of an unknown (to us) author, whose book he threw down in a rage. Now he gathered up the scattered materials of *Bracebridge Hall* and fashioned them into the first of the Leather-Stocking Tales (in order of composition), *The Pioneers* (1823).

Cooper was able to use characters, situations, and names from Irving's fiction because he had himself known an American version of squirarchy. His father, William Cooper, dominated Cooperstown, New York, which he had founded, and ran the town on rigorous Federalist principles. [12] Judge Marmaduke Temple of Templeton is, as every critic of *The Pioneers* has noted, based on

William Cooper. He is the representative of order, stability, continuity, society itself.

His antagonist is Natty Bumppo, who became, in subsequent tales, the greatest American embodiment of what D. H. Lawrence has called "the spirit of the place." Robert Zoellner has noted that Natty is an ambiguous figure whose noble sentiments are qualified by runny nose, snaggled tooth, and faulty syntax.[13] But Judge Temple is quite as ambiguously characterized. His moral position—like the portico of his mansion—is embarrassingly unsteady.

The pretentious portico is given a long paragraph in Chapter 5 of *The Pioneers:*

> The foundations actually left the superstructure suspended in the air, leaving an open space of a foot between the base of the pillars to the stones on which they had originally been placed. It was lucky . . . that the carpenter . . . had fastened the canopy of this classic entrance so firmly to the side of the house, that, when the base deserted the superstructure . . . and the pillars . . . were no longer of service to support the roof, the roof was able to uphold the pillars.

Cooper had already ridiculed the building's lines; he further undermines Judge Temple's position by describing the furnishings. Although Judge Temple, modeled on Cooper's father, is meant to be a sympathetic figure, his home is cluttered by the meaningless relics of misunderstood tradition:

> On . . . pedestals were small busts in blacked plaster of Paris. . . . On one stood Homer, a most striking likeness, Richard affirmed, "as any one might see, for it was blind." Another bore the image of a smooth visaged gentleman, with a pointed beard, whom he called Shakespeare, A third ornament was an urn . . . intended to represent itself as holding the ashes of Dido. A fourth was certainly old Franklin, in his cap and spectacles. A fifth as surely bore the dignified composure of the face of Washington. A sixth was a nondescript, representing "a man with a shirt-collar open," to use the language of

Richard, "with a laurel on his head;—it was Julius Caesar or
Dr. Faustus; there were good reasons for believing either."

Had the Leather-Stocking Tales been Cooper's only work,
we should be justified in classifying him among rebels against
civilization. But the Tales are only a part of the Cooper canon.
The pugnacious American, who chastized Irving for his "descants
upon the . . . dignity of descent," voyaged to Europe, criticized
in three novels the feudal institutions he found there,[14] and returned to the United States, in 1833, to discover that American
democracy was less satisfactory than he remembered it.[15] The
optimism of *Notions of the Americans* (1828) gave way to the
doubts of *The American Democrat* (1838), in which Cooper
denounces the veniality of the press, the power of demagogues
over public opinion, and the incivilities of American deportment.
The barrage was followed up by a heavy shelf of novels designed
to crush the follies of equalitarianism and to reveal anew the
truth of Revelation.[16]

Some of the novels are tendentious claptrap; others are among
the best Cooper ever wrote. Most important of the polemical
books are the three novels which comprise the Littlepage Manuscripts. In them, Cooper affirms the values of a European order
based on hereditary land ownership.

Cornelius Littlepage, the founder of the line, is born at Satans-
toe, the Westchester mansion that gives a title to the first novel
of the trilogy. Keenly aware of the importance of property,
Corny marries Anneke Mordaunt—and wins her vast estates.
Among these estates is Herman Mordaunt's blockhouse in upper New York. The blockhouse is the germ of a manorial settlement. Corny Littlepage defends Ravensnest from the raiding
parties of the French and Indian War. His son, Mordaunt Littlepage, in *The Chainbearer,* preserves the property from the un-
scrupulous machinations of Jason Newcome, a disloyal lawyer
who aligns himself with squatters to the detriment of the Littlepage interests. Cooper's conservative bent is apparent in his sly
use of significant names (such as "Newcome") and in his *obiter
dicta:*

All the knowledge, and all the arts of life that the white man
enjoys and turns to his profit [explains Mordaunt to the Indian
Susquesas], come from the rights of property. No man would
build a wigwam to make rifles in, if he thought he could not
keep it as long as he wished, sell it when he pleased, and leave
it to his son. . . .

Ravensnest is the symbol of these rights. In the last novel, *The
Redskins,* Hugh Littlepage (Mordaunt's grandson) rushes home
from Paris to defend his estates against the anti-rent mobs which
terrorized New York's patroons in the 1840's. The agitation is
led by Seneca Newcome, the rascally grandson of Jason Newcome.
Seneca's perfidy is dramatized in his attempt to burn the house.
Foiled in this, he sets the turbulent townspeople, disguised as
"Redskins," marching on Ravensnest. By an ironic twist, the
Littlepages rely upon real Indians to rescue the house. Aged
Susquesas remembers Mordaunt's sermon on property rights:
"No red man wants another's wigwam. If he wants a wigwam,
he builds one himself. It is not so with the pale-faces. The man
who has no wigwam tries to get away his neighbor's." Susquesas
saves the Littlepages' "wigwam."

It would, however, be incorrect to say that the house is the
dominant symbol of the Littlepage Manuscripts. Cooper was
not the artist to elaborate patterns of imagery. Hawthorne was.
In *The House of the Seven Gables,* Hawthorne consciously ma-
nipulates the symbolism of the house.[17] The Pyncheon house
stands as a token of the Pyncheons' past. The past is, moreover,
an evil one, for the land beneath the house was stolen from
Matthew Maule, whom Colonel Pyncheon had falsely accused of
witchcraft. Holgrave, deguerreotypist and reformer, wants to
demolish the house and to begin anew. He wants to tear down
"the moss-grown and rotten Past." He argues that "The house
. . . is expressive of that odious and abominable Past, with all its
bad influences, against which I have just been declaiming. I dwell
in it for a while, that I may know the better how to hate it."
Convinced that all of us "live in dead men's houses," Holgrave

urges that "no man . . . build his house for posterity. . . . If each generation were allowed and expected to build its own houses, that single change . . . would imply almost every reform which society is now suffering for. I doubt whether even our public edifices—our capitols, state-houses, court-houses, city-hall, and churches—ought to be built of such permanent materials as stone or brick." Holgrave suggests that "it were better that they should crumble to ruin once in twenty years . . . as a hint to the people to examine into and reform the institutions which they symbolize."

But Hawthorne is not of Holgrave's opinion. Weak-witted Clifford Pyncheon, fleeing madly from the mansion, condemns it as representative of the past, and seems thereby to parody Holgrave's radicalism. Clifford rides the railroad and declaims that there "is no such unwholesome atmosphere as that of an old home, rendered poisonous by one's defunct forefathers. . . ." He describes his seven-gabled ancestral place as a "rusty, crazy, creaky, dry-rotted, damp-rotted, dingy, dark, and miserable old dungeon. . . ." If only it could be "torn down," or "burnt up, and so the earth be rid of it, and grass be sown abundantly over its foundation." But, at the end of his ride, Clifford finds "a wooden church, black with age, and in a dismal state of ruin and decay, with broken windows, a great rift through the main body of the edifice, and a rafter dangling from the top of the square tower." Beyond are uninhabited houses. Realizing that he cannot flee from society or from the past, Clifford returns home. "A dreary home," he says to Hepzibah, "But you have done well to bring me hither." Despite Maule's curse, it is *his* house, and it contains happy memories as well as sad ones.

We are not surprised at Clifford's return, but Holgrave's conversion shocks us. He wins Phoebe Pyncheon, accepts the past, and suggests that "domestic architecture in stone, rather than in wood," would be the thing after all. It would give "that impression of permanence . . . essential to the happiness of any one moment." Phoebe is astounded by this change of heart, but Hawthorne was true to himself when he turned Holgrave from his radicalism.

One great story by Hawthorne, "My Kinsman, Major Molineux," turns on the American Revolution. Viewed psychologically, it is a *rite de passage* from innocence to experience; viewed politically, it is a somber affirmation of independence from the past, a Puritan's version of "Rip Van Winkle." But most of Hawthorne's work is more Conservative.[18] It was Hawthorne's conviction, expressed in "Earth's Holocaust" and elsewhere, that the human heart itself is the root of all evil. The past is wicked because men are wicked. We inherit the evil our fathers did, and we do evil ourselves.

Hester Prynne defies magistrates and ministers and says to Arthur Dimmesdale, "What we did had a consecration of its own," but Hawthorne's sympathy is not tantamount to his approval. He rebukes his heroine when she thinks of suicide ("The scarlet letter had not done its office") and, when she rips the symbol from her breast, he uses little Pearl to remind her that primitivistic rebellion is incompatible with civilized life. The consequences of past actions are always present. Hester accepts her responsibilities and society's judgment, until acceptance demonstrates that society judged too quickly. Except to dogmatic Liberalism, the end is no more a puzzle than the end of *The House of the Seven Gables* or of Henry James's *Portrait of a Lady*.

Hawthorne could not bring himself unreservedly to admire England,[19] and his attempts to make a novel of the materials of English notebooks led only to fragments. (The Text of *Dr. Grimshawe's Secret,* which Hawthorne never finished, contains this remark by Hawthorne's returned American hero: "Oh home, my home, my forefather's home! I have come back to thee! The wanderer has come back!" And, shortly after, this interpolation by Hawthorne: "What unimaginable nonsense!"[20])

Neither could Hawthorne bring himself to celebrate the two great contradictory American myths—the myth of Eden (which he repudiated in *The Marble Faun*) and the myth of Utopia (which he put aside in *The Blithedale Romance* and in "The Celestial Railway"). History cannot be evaded by a return to primitivism nor by the inauguration of the millennium. We do well to accept our fate, to link hands in "the magnetic chain of humanity," or—to change back to the basic metaphor—to dwell together in our fathers' house.

Henry James preferred *The House of the Seven Gables* to his predecessor's other work. The preference is appropriate, for James shared many of Hawthorne's concerns. Like Hawthorne, James came to feel that it was a "complex fate" to be an American.[21] In the first volume of his autobiography, *A Small Boy and Others,* he told how, as a child, he had looked up a village street, seen a peasant in sabots and a ruined castle in the distance, and realized what Europe meant to him:

> Europe mightn't have flattered, it was true, at my finding her thus most signified and summarised in a sordid old woman scraping a mean living and an uninhabitable tower abandoned to the owls; that was but the momentary measure of a small sick boy, however, the virtue of the impression was proportioned to my capacity. It made a bridge over to more things than I then knew.

The metaphor of the bridge is apt for one who spent his early manhood in anxious passage back and forth between the Old World and the New.

Arriving in London in 1872 (not, of course, for the first time), James felt that "all history appeared to live again, and the continuity of things to vibrate through my mind." But a moment later came the "tiger-pounce of homesickness." [22] American or European? His debts to Emerson and Hawthorne (and his Swedenborgian father) are immense; his apprenticeship to the French realists and to Turgenev is as important. He was a passionate pilgrim to the shrine of Europe—so passionate that his adoration of the Old World exasperated even Mrs. Henry Adams, who complained in her diary, "It is high time Harry

James was ordered home by his family. He is too good a fellow to be spoiled by injudicious old ladies in London—and in the long run they would like him all the better for knowing and loving his own country. He had better go to Cheyenne and run a hog ranch." [23]

Innumerable critics have examined the European and the American in him, and concluded that James always qualified his enthusiasms.[24] Perhaps the simplest answer is to say that James solved the problem of identity in the manner of one who truly believed that "art . . . *makes* life"; [25] he dramatized the "international theme" in his novels and dwelled as much in the house of fiction as in any other home.

Art makes life, but art needs a great deal of life to work upon. In his study of Hawthorne, James wrote that "the flower of art blooms only where the soil is deep, that it takes a great deal of history to produce a little literature, that it needs a complex social machinery to set a writer in motion." James, in the second chapter, quoted the preface to *The Marble Faun,* in which Hawthorne remarked the "difficulty of writing a romance about a country where there is no shadow, no antiquity, no mystery, no picturesque and gloomy wrong. . . ." James's account of what is, indeed, absent from the "texture of American life" is a catalogue of the elements of a Conservative society:

> No State, in the European sense of the word. . . . No sovereign, no court, no personal loyalty, no aristocracy, no church, no clergy, no army, no diplomatic service, no country gentlemen, no palaces, no castles, nor manors, nor old country houses, nor parsonages, nor thatched cottages, nor ivied ruins; no cathedrals, nor abbeys, nor little Norman churches; no great universities, nor public schools—no Oxford, nor Eton, nor Harrow. . . .*

---

* Three years later, in his story, "The Point of View," James took sentiments like these, exaggerated them, and came up with a European's doleful response to Washington, D.C.: "No movement, no officials, no authority, no embodiment of the State. Enormous streets, *comme toujours,* lined with little red houses where nothing ever passes but the tramway. The Capitol—a vast structure, false

America had many attractions, and the comic sense that James alluded to is one of them, but there was no substitute for "troublesome history, for the long, the immitigable process of time." [26] Europe had the "palpable, imaginable *visitable* past." [27]

James is one who visited, and stayed. Ralph Pendrel, the hero of *The Sense of the Past,* is another. Pendrel, who resembles the characters that Hawthorne invented in the anguish and confusion of his last, unfinished romances, is a novelist who has inherited "an old house, a piece of suggestive concrete antiquity." A friend reminds Pendrel that he had used the phrase, "the sense of the past," as "the thing in life you desired most to arrive at." She quotes from Pendrel's book: "There are particular places where things have happened, places enclosed and ordered and subject to the continuity of life. . . ." The inherited house is all that Pendrel could have hoped it to be. Entering the house on a rainy afternoon, he discovers it to be "a museum of held reverberations." Pendrel moves, magically, into the past, and there we leave him, for *The Sense of the Past* is one of James's unfinished novels.

Many readers have complained about the way in which we take leave of Isabel Archer, but *The Portrait of a Lady* is—so far as James was concerned—complete. Her career takes her from "an old house at Albany" to Gardencourt to the Palazzo Roccanera. The house in Albany is, in many ways, the most curious. Isabel Archer's particular sanctuary is a "mysterious apartment which lay beyond the library and which was called, traditionally, no one knew why, the office." There is a door to the street, but this door is barred and "secured by bolts which a particularly slender little girl found . . . impossible to slide." The door opened "into the street; if the sidelights had not been filled with green paper she might have looked out upon the little brown

classic, white marble, iron and stucco. . . . You go into the Capitol as you would into a rail-way station; you walk about as you would in the Palais Royal. No functionaries, no door-keepers, no officers, no uniforms, no badges, no reservations, no authority—nothing but a crowd of shabby people circulating in a labyrinth of spittoons."

stoop and the well-worn brick pavement. But she had no wish to look out, for this would have interfered with her theory that there was a strange, unseen place on the other side—a place which became to the child's imagination, according to its different moods, a region of delight or of terror." In Gardencourt, Isabel discovered delight. It is a lovely English country-house, imposingly situated:

> It stood upon a low hill, above the river—the river being the Thames at some forty miles from London. A long gabled front of red brick, with the complexion of which time and the weather had played all sorts of pictorial tricks, only, however, to improve and refine it, presented to the lawn its patches of ivy, its clustered chimneys, its windows smothered in creepers. The house had a name and a history. . . .

Ralph Touchett tells Isabel, when she asks if the "romantic old house" has a ghost, that Gardencourt is "dismally prosaic" and ghostless. Isabel, who is often called naïve by literary historians, is right; sophisticated Ralph is wrong. At the end of the novel, on the night of Ralph's death, Isabel finds the ghost:

> She heard no knock, but at the time the darkness began vaguely to grow grey she started up from her pillow as abruptly as if she had received a summons. It seemed to her for an instant that he was standing there—a vague, hovering figure in the vagueness of the room. She stared a moment; she saw his white face—his kind eyes; then she saw there was nothing.

But there *was* something. Human society is a good mixed inextricably with evil. All our houses are haunted. Unfortunately for Isabel, she had ventured from the house in Albany only to return in the end to another house more restrictive. After the delight had come the terror.

The fourth house, the one in which she is doomed to dwell, is Gilbert Osmond's Roman palazzo—a kind of heightened representative of the haunted house. Like the house in Albany, it is shut off from the world. Osmond's Florentine villa foreshadows the palazzo. It is entirely enclosed:

> The windows of the ground-floor . . . were, in their noble proportions, extremely architectural; but their function seemed less to offer communication with the world than to defy the world to look in. They were massively cross-barred, and placed at such a height that curiosity, even on tiptoe, expired before it reached them.

His Roman palace is a prison. As Isabel's situation worsens, the walls of the house seem to close in upon her. Osmond had at first appeared "a man living in the open air of the world," but "in the mansion of his own habitation" Isabel saw him as he really was. James describes not Osmond but the house:

> It was the house of darkness, the house of dumbness, the house of suffocation. Osmond's beautiful mind gave it neither light nor air; Osmond's beautiful mind indeed seemed to peep down from a small high window and mock at her.

Isabel moves in the end from nature to civilization, from a dreadful freedom to an endurable thralldom. The metaphors tell the story: "The world . . . had never seemed so large; it seemed to open out, all round her, to take the form of a mighty sea, where she floated in fathomless waters." Kissed by Caspar Goodwood, who begs her to flee with him, Isabel has a presentiment of drowning. She turns to the house and to Osmond:

> There were lights in the windows of the house; they shone far across the lawn. In an extraordinarily short time . . . she had moved through the darkness (for she saw nothing) and reached the door. Here only she paused. She looked all about her; she listened a little; then she put her hand on the latch. She had not known where to turn; but she knew now. There was a very straight path.

Well might she pause, for the return is through the pathless darkness. Perhaps the lights in the windows promise something. The reader can only speculate. The novel ends with Isabel's

return to Osmond's mansion, and with Henrietta Stackpole hand-
ing Caspar Goodwood the "key to patience." The reader, lacking
Henrietta's optimism and Caspar's endurance, is sure that no key
of his will ever unlock Isabel Archer's doors. Whether she goes
back because of her promise to Pansy or because of her conception of duty or because of her fears of drowning in a sea of unfamiliar experience, Isabel goes back. She wanted to choose her
fate and she did. It is as though James were telling us that the
barred door of the house in Albany opened upon a road that led
to Gardencourt *and* to the Palazzo Roccanera, to terror *and* delight. James agreed with Hawthorne. The plans for the Perfect
House are, like the dream of Eden, visionary, but the lights of a
haunted house are to be preferred to the darkness outside.

It is a grim message for a book that is, in many of its moments,
comic.[28] Isable Archer's fate foreshadows that of other Jamesian
heroes and heroines who discover that Emersonian self-reliance
is not enough in the moral labyrinth of European society,[29] but
even the briefest discussion of James and the Conservative imagination should leave room for a paragraph about the last
and greatest of his novels.

The Golden Bowl repeats the *donnée* of *Portrait of a Lady*.
Maggie Verver, appropriately named for a vivacious American
girl, begins in innocence: "Oh," she exclaims, "I'm not afraid of
history!" She marries a comparatively impoverished Italian prince,
a man infinitely wise in the ways of traditional society, a man
willing to accept a little ingenuousness in return for a lovely
wife and a lot of money. The marriage is flawed, like the golden
bowl which Maggie receives as a wedding present. The prince has
continued an affair with her best friend (who married Maggie's
father in order to be near the prince). In a dramatic war of wills,
fought most intensely at Fawns, another mansion symbolic of
society itself, Maggie proves herself the master of the most intri-
cate strategies of European manners. She is strong and still compassionate. She triumphs, sends her rival off to America, and
proves that Conservatism is not always synonymous with the loss

of freedom suffered by Isabel Archer. The "ordeal of conscious-ness" is strenuous, but, for the rich, for the talented, for those who play the game with sufficient skill, the rewards are immense.*

2 A Past of Our Own

In our literary histories, James is likely to be paired with Howells, while Hawthorne is paired with Faulkner. The first two are "Realists" concerned with the "novel," while the second two are "Romanticists" concerned with the "romance." If, however, we look at the image of the house, and at the thematic implications of that image, we arrange our authors somewhat differently. James and Hawthorne are very similar in their sense of the past; Faulkner, despite his talk of the Civil War, gradually came to resemble Howells. Like Howells, Faulkner was interested not in the rediscovery but in the creation of social order. Ralph Pendrel and Isabel Archer and Phoebe Pyncheon find houses; Thomas Sutpen and Flem Snopes and Silas Lapham build them.

In the *Atlantic Monthly* for February 1880, Howells reviewed his friend's book on Hawthorne and differed sharply with him on the "texture of American life." [30] Howells considered James's list of absent items and pronounced them "dreary and worn-out paraphernalia" that Hawthorne was better off without. What have we left if we have not the "manners, customs, usages, habits, forms" [31] of European civilization? "We have simply the whole of human life left." We have, for instance, the world of business enterprise and the adventures of a middle-aged man from the provinces, the "new man" of the 1880's, Silas Lapham, who

* Rich, talented, skillful Edith Wharton, whose admirers claim for her an originality not revealed in her books, shared her mentor's sense of the past. The hero of *Hudson River Bracketed,* a young booby reared in Pruneville, Advance, Euphoria, Hallelujah and other odd places, discovers a symbolic mansion to instruct him in "the incomprehensible past" (which resembles Wharton's own past as described in her autobiography, *A Backward Glance*). *The Age of Innocence* is the best of her mannered dramas of the old and the new rich. In our own day, Mrs. Wharton's work has been continued by her great admirer, Louis Auchincloss.

thinks he would like to build a grand new house in the grand old style.[32]

Although Silas Lapham's new house on Beacon Street is the dominant symbol of *The Rise of Silas Lapham,* there are actually three houses which characterize their owners and their owners' aspirations: Coreys' house on Beacon Street, the Laphams' house on Nankeen Square, and the new mansion on Beacon Street. The house on Nankeen Square is the urban equivalent of Marmaduke Temple's mansion:

> In the panelled spaces on the walls were some stone-coloured landscapes, representing the mountains and cañons of the West. . . . In front of the long windows . . . were statues, kneeling figures which turned their backs upon the company . . . and represented allegories of Faith and Prayer. . . . A white marble group of several figures, expressing an Italian conception of Lincoln Freeing the Slaves,—a Latin negro and his wife,—with our Eagle flapping his wings in approval, at Lincoln's feet, occupied one corner, and balanced the what-not of an earlier period in another.

Silas Lapham can manufacture the house paint essential to urban life, but he cannot achieve the urbanities of life in society. The Coreys' house on Beacon Street, opposite the Common, is quite another matter. It had "a wooden portico, with slender fluted columns . . . painted white, and which, with the delicate mouldings of the cornice, form the sole and sufficient decoration of the street front; nothing could be simpler, and nothing could be better." If the Laphams' house is an expression of their vulgarity, the Coreys' house objectifies their taste and breeding.

More important than either is the house which Silas Lapham builds. It is the emblem of his rise into the upper-class society of Beacon Hill. Knowing that property symbolizes propriety, he invests the house with all his aspirations—and with far too much of his fortune. Silas is putty in the hands of a professional architect. His dream of a brownstone finished in black walnut is re-designed into a country house with low-studded entrance story, high parlors, white paint, "a little gold here and there" and "a painted frieze round under the cornice—garlands of roses on a gold ground. . . ." Silas is converted to the "Ongpeer" style.

Mrs. Lapham is not converted. She broods over a bit of sharp trading which was the basis for the Lapham fortune. She seems to feel the hand of Nemesis on the drawing board. The chapter, filled with Silas's enthusiasm for the house, closes with an echo of Maule's curse: "And don't you ask me," says Mrs. Lapham, "to go to that house with you. . . . You can sell it, for all me. I sha'n't live in it. There's blood on it." Although Howells avoids "the boscage of the supernatural," the house is, in fact, destroyed.

Dismayed by business difficulties and by his dismal showing at the Coreys' dinner party, Silas retreats alone to the unfinished house. He peers from the window:

> The Cambridge flats showed the sad, sodden yellow of mead-ows stripped bare after a long sleep under snow; the hills, the naked trees, the spires and roofs had a black outline, as if they were objects in a landscape of the French school.

The landscape, like the house, is art, and there is no comfort in it. Silas tests the chimney and carelessly sets fire to the house. It burns to the ground. Silas is ruined, economically and socially. His moral rise—his refusal to cheat, a second time, in business—takes him back to Vermont, back to begin the world anew where he had first begun it, in the hills of Lapham.

> He put the house at Nankeen Square . . . into the payment of his debts, and Mrs. Lapham found it easier to leave it for the old farmstead in Vermont than it would have been to go from that home . . . to the new house on the water side of Beacon.

But Penelope Lapham does marry Tom Corey. After all, this is a novel about the land of opportunity and—to use a newer phrase —social mobility. Howells was what James aptly called him, the novelist of "the real, the natural, the colloquial, the moderate, the optimistic, the domestic, and the democratic." [33] He remained a Liberal until the social injustice of the age turned him to Christian Socialism.

William Faulkner might have been the Christian that Hyatt Waggoner and Cleanth Brooks make him out to be,[34] but he was certainly too much of a romantic individualist to qualify as a socialist. His romanticism was tied up with his sense of the past, whose present ramifications were an obsessive theme in his fiction. He felt his fate as a Southerner to be complex and tragic when he did not feel it charged with explosively comic potentialities.

The continuity of families in time is so important to the Yoknapatawpha Saga that critical studies come equipped with genealogical charts and essays on affiliation. The decline and fall of Faulkner's families has been studied as closely as if we were all involved in their destiny, but room remains, nonetheless, for comments on two families not usually thought to resemble each other—the Sutpens and the Snopeses.

Colonel Lapham, like Colonel Pyncheon, found his family fortunes linked—or should one say mortised and tenoned—to a house. The rise and fall of Colonel Thomas Sutpen, the tragic hero of Faulkner's *Absalom, Absalom!,* also parallels the construction and the destruction of a mansion (and the rise and fall of the plantation South). Colonel Sutpen arrives in Yoknapatawpha County—no one knows his origins—and proceeds to build his house. We discover that he builds in emulation of the plantation house of a Virginia planter who had scornfully directed him to the servants' door.

The people of Jefferson, amazed and awed, "would sit in a curious quiet clump as though for mutual protection and watch his mansion rise, carried plank by plank and brick by brick out of the swamp where the clay and timber waited. . . ." Sutpen is clearly a driven man, and the house is meant as a sanctuary. The travails of the captive French architect are a comic measurement of the length to which Sutpen will go. As Shreve says to Quentin

Compson, Sutpen was a kind of rural Faustus who "appeared suddenly one Sunday . . . and skulldugged a hundred miles of land out of a poor ignorant Indian and built the biggest house on it you ever saw and went away with six wagons and came back with the crystal tapestries and the Wedgwood chairs to furnish it and nobody knew if he had robbed another steamboat or had just dug up a little more of the old loot. . . ."

Sutpen's ambition is to build a house in the metaphoric as well as in the literal sense. He wants sons and grandsons, a family in the Conservative sense, a "line." But his house is cursed. It is built upon the evil of slavery. Sutpen's affairs are as complicated as those of King David, whose lament for his son gives the book its allusive title. Charles Bon, Sutpen's illegitimate son, has Negro blood. When Henry Sutpen, the legitimate scion, discovers this, he kills Charles Bon and thus prevents him from marrying Judith Sutpen. Henry disappears and his father attempts to have legitimate male children by the granddaughter of a servant. The baby is female. Sutpen scorns the child and is killed by the outraged retainer. The fall of the house of Sutpen, in the literal sense, comes in 1910, when Henry returns to die in the house his father built. Clytemnestra Sutpen, Henry's illegitimate, half-Negro sister, sets fire to the mansion. It burns to the ground, and no Sutpen is left—except for Charles Bon's idiot grandson, Jim Bond, who wanders howling about the ashes of the house.

Had Faulkner written only of the Sutpens and the Sartorises and the Compsons (whose house is burned by *their* idiot son), his novels would be a gloomy prophecy. Fortunately, there are the Snopeses to suggest that the doom of Conservativism need not mean the end of all hope.

The rise of Flem Snopes is dramatized by the movement from the hamlet to the town, from the shack to the mansion that represents domination of the town. Having conquered Frenchman's Bend, Flem Snopes moves to Jefferson, and there he determines to build his house, with "colyums" so that "even a feller that never seen colyums before wouldn't have no doubt a-tall what they was, like in the photographs where the Confedrit sweetheart in a hoop skirt and a magnolia is saying good-bye to her Confedrit beau jest before he rides off to finish tending to General Grant. . . ." The house, with its ostentatiously ante-bellum columns, is Flem's substitute for a family tree. Since Flem is sexually impotent, the house will have to serve as progeny as well. The last novel of the trilogy, appropriately entitled *The Mansion,* carries Flem's project through to completion. Major De Spain's mansion is rebuilt by Flem as the visible symbol of his conquest of Jefferson.

> Anybody that had or could think up the occasion, could pass along the street and watch Wat and his work gang of kinfolks and in-laws tearing off Major De Spain's front gallery and squaring up the back of the house and building and setting up them colyums to reach all the way from the ground up to the second-storey roof, until even when the painting was finished it still wouldn't be as big as Mount Vernon of course, but then Mount Vernon was a thousand miles away so there wasn't no chance of invidious or malicious eye-to-eye comparison.

V. K. Ratliff, who narrates this section of *The Mansion,* is not satisfied with the allusion to George Washington. He suggests that the house might have been, for all it changed Flem, "the solid ancestral symbol of Alexander Hamilton and Aaron Burr and Astor and Morgan and Harriman and Hill and ever other golden advocate of hard quick-thinking vested interest. . . ."

But Flem's career is not a steady rise. Like Silas Lapham, he had done wrong. In this case, the wrong was done to Mink Snopes (who had been jailed because Flem didn't save him). Mink kills Flem. The house becomes a mausoleum. It remains, with its absurd "colyums," as a monument to the comic hero, as a more than momentary stay against confusion.

The difference between the stories of Thomas Sutpen and Flem

Snopes is partly that between tragedy and comedy, but there is also the possibility of a change in Faulkner's attitude toward the family that entered *Sartoris* as symbols of degradation. Between *Sartoris,* published in 1929, and *The Mansion,* published in 1959, came the Great Depression and a war more frightful than either the Civil War or World War I. Paradoxically, Faulkner seems more hopeful in 1959.

It may well be that Faulkner is closer to Conservatism than to any other paradigm of social organization, but the case will have to be made with account taken of the Faustian drive of his Sutpens and his Snopeses. Defiance of social norms, a tendency to violence, and an obsessive, reckless, ruthless ambition are not the characteristics usually associated with Conservatism.

Colonel Sutpen's mansion burned, and Silas Lapham's hopes were buried in the ashes of his house on Beacon Street. One might extend a dour monologue with talk of the House of Usher's "mighty walls rushing asunder" and with dismal references to the "decayed house" of Eliot's "Gerontion" and to the fire that destroyed James's Poynton. But Ravensnest and the House of the Seven Gables and Gardencourt and Flem Snopes's Mansion still stand to affirm the possibility of permanence and the values of society. The virgin land no longer forms the democratic vista. We have Pittsburgh and Chicago and Cape Kennedy; we also have Paul Revere's house in Boston and Longfellow's in Cambridge, Byrd's Westover and Jefferson's Monticello. Although Louis Sullivan offices and Frank Lloyd Wright homes continue to fall to the bulldozers of Progress, the magnificent façade of the Boston State House has been newly renovated and Americans have made a shrine even of Henry Thoreau's anti-house at Walden Pond. Considering the misconceptions of popular history, one might almost say that we have an imaginary past with real houses in it.

One of these real houses belonged to Edward Dickinson, Treasurer of Amherst College and father of a poet. Richard Wilbur's poem is not too long to quote:

ALTITUDES *

I

Look up into the dome:
It is a great salon, a brilliant place,
    Yet not too splendid for the race
Whom we imagine there, wholly at home

    With the gold-rosetted white
Wainscot, the oval windows, and the fault-
    Less figures of the painted vault.
Strolling, conversing in that precious light,

    They chat no doubt of love,
The pleasant burden of their courtesy
    Borne down at times to you and me
Where, in this dark, we stand and gaze above.

    For all they cannot share,
All that the world cannot in fact afford,
    Their lofty premises are floored
With the massed voices of continual prayer.

II

How far it is from here
To Emily Dickinson's father's house in America;
    Think of her climbing a spiral stair
Up to the little cupola with its clear

    Small panes, its room for one.
Like the dark house below, so full of eyes
    In mirrors and of shut-in flies,
This chamber furnished only with the sun

Is she and she alone,
A mood to which she rises, in which she sees
Bird-choristers in all the trees
And a wild shining of the pure unknown

On Amherst. This is caught
In the dormers of a neighbor, who, no doubt,
Will before long be coming out
To pace about his garden, lost in thought.

The theme, clearly, is one of contrast. Saint Peter's on the one hand, and Emily Dickinson's father's house on the other. The huddled Faithful at Mass are compressed into a pun, but they, at the bottom of the first section, "floor" the splendid race that dwells among the "gold-rosetted white Wainscot" and the oval windows of the dome. The god-like figures' talk is only intermittently borne down to the Americans standing in the darkness of the cathedral. The first half of the poem is an architectural statement of hierarchy in society and gradation in the divine order of things.

It is very different in America. One climbs from the dark house below to the cupola. The "opulent sun" that smears Wallace Stevens's "shuttered mansion-house" furnishes the spare world of Emily Dickinson's chamber.[35] Enclosed and alone, Emily Dickinson looks out at the "bird-choristers" and at "a wild shining of the pure unknown | On Amherst." Then, in the complex compromise of the poem, the "pure unknown" is qualified by the reflections caught in the dormers of the house next door. Wilbur imagines Emily Dickinson as she watches a neighbor, lost in *his* private world of shrubbery and thought. Perhaps the poem is Wilbur's way of saying that America does have a past. We do have our houses now, and our traditions. One cannot be a Conservative without a sense of the past, but one can have a sense of the past without becoming a Conservative. Conservatives are not the only Americans with poets to cherish and shrines to visit.

America still lacks palaces and castles and manors and thatched cottages and ivied ruins, but the high hedge and white cupola of Emily Dickinson's house, and the "Called Back" of her tombstone, seem—in a chauvinistic mood—alternative enough.

III

The Establishment of Religion *

1 *Orestes Brownson and the Conservative Theory of Church and State*

Religion, in the traditional sense that excludes secular faith, is very high on the list of Conservative principles. "We know, and, what is better, we feel inwardly," wrote Burke in the *Reflections,* that "religion is the basis of civil authority. . . . We know, and it is our pride to know, that man is by his constitution a religious animal. . . ." Twentieth-century scholars readily assent: Conservatives are religious.[1] But religious men are not necessarily Conservative. This is a truth that can scarcely be overstated.

Unquestionably, there is an element of traditionalism in Christianity. Christians orient themselves by reference to historical actions that are believed to make manifest the will of God as revealed to His chosen people and as displayed by the life and death of His only Son. Christian rituals re-enact moments in time which are considered by the believer to be timeless in their significance. There is, moreover, an element of authoritarianism in Christian-

* An earlier version of this essay appeared as "From Brownson to Eliot: The Conservative Theory of Church and State," *American Quarterly,* XVII (1965), 483–500.

ity. The Jewish concept of a patriarchal deity and the Christian concept of piety have political implications which Conservative thinkers have frequently emphasized. Conservatives have equated obedience to God's commands and obedience to constituted political authority. In practice, that which is rendered to God is similar to if not identical with that which is rendered to Caesar.

But Judaism and Christianity have prophetic traditions as well as priestly ones. There is in both faiths an inherent and theologically justified tendency to procure challengers as well as maintainers of order, levelers as well as defenders of hierarchy, heralds of the new as well as sanctifiers of the old. Without the institutional framework of a church, Christians are likely to approach their heritage selectively and to derive radical rather than Conservative conclusions from the Old Testament and, *a fortiori,* from the New. The history of Fundamentalism in America indicates that Biblical faith is often conservative (i.e. reluctant to accept change) but seldom if ever Conservative.

It is simply not helpful to be told, as Russell Kirk tells his readers, that "freedom is submission to the will of God" unless there is an authoritative institution to interpret God's will. Unless such an institution exists, individuals are likely to strike out on their own in response to eccentric interpretations of Holy Writ or even in answer to "special revelations."

Many are the American radicals, from the days of Anne Hutchinson and Roger Williams to those of Willard Uphaus and Martin Luther King, whose Christian commitments led them where no Conservative can follow. The example of William Lloyd Garrison ought to be enough in itself to upset the easy assumption that religion and Conservatism are positively correlated.

Belief in Original Sin, which is almost always part of the Conservative credo, is without political consequences. Original Sin leads to Conservative theory only when two conditions are met: (1) when one believes that some men are exempted by Grace or some other means from the effects of the Fall, and (2) when one also believes that the exempted can be separated, for political purposes, from the "unregenerate." [2] But the separation must be institutionalized and the obvious means is the Church, which interprets the decisions of the Almighty and rejects the sinner's claim.

Burke himself was very clear on the uselessness of "religion" without the proper institutional forms. Closely paraphrasing Hooker's *Ecclesiastical Polity,* he insisted that "in a Christian commonwealth the Church and the State are one and the same thing, being different integral parts of the same whole." [3] He wrote, in one of the most ardent sections of the *Reflections,* "He who gave our nature to be perfected by our virtue willed also the necessary means of its perfection: He willed, therefore, the state: He willed its connection with the source and original archetype of all perfection." The institutional form of this connection was, of course, the "Church Establishment" that Burke defended as "the first of our prejudices." Englishmen, he continued, "do not consider their Church establishment as convenient, but as essential to their state: not as a thing heterogeneous and separable,— something added for accommodation. . . . They consider it as the foundation of their whole Constitution, with which, and with every part of which, it holds an indissoluble union. Church and State are ideas inseparable in their minds. . . ." The necessity of establishment was never doubted by Burke.[4] It was never doubted by his great coadjutor on the continent, Joseph de Maistre:

> The excellence and durability of great political institutions are proportionate to the closeness of the union of politics and religion within them. . . . There should be a state religion just as there is a state political system; or rather, religious and political dogmas, mingled and merged together, should form a *general* or *national mind* sufficiently strong to repress the aberrations of the individual reason which is, of its nature, the mortal enemy of any association whatever because it gives birth only to divergent opinions.[5]

The necessity for establishment was certainly never doubted by Pope Leo XIII, the great nineteenth-century formulator of Catholic theory of Church and State.

American Conservatives loyal to Burkean ideals and American Catholics faithful to Leo's encyclicals have hewn to this line. They have, however, been frustrated by the First Amendment to the Constitution and by the commitment of most Protestants and Jews to religious voluntarism.[6] Since the early nineteenth-century disestablishments of the Congregational Church in New England, the trend has been away from the kind of church that Burke and Leo XIII thought indispensable to a Conservative society menaced by the age of the democratic revolution. The extraordinary thing about the Conservative theory of Church and State is that it has been maintained in America only by one substantial thinker, Orestes Brownson, and by an ever-smaller like-minded minority within his Church.

The Puritans of Massachusetts Bay prefigured, in their wilderness Zion, Burke's insistence on the close connection of Church and State, and Jonathan Boucher held that "No other form of church-government than that of the Church of England would be compatible with the form of our civil government," [7] but the American Revolution put an end, politically, to the possibility of an established church. The so-called "establishment" in New England was not really what Burke and other Conservatives meant. The New England system stipulated taxation for the support of Christian ministers. Timothy Dwight, crusty old Federalist that he was, insisted that "establishment" really meant "The legal establishment of the public worship of God." [8] No Church was authoritative in relation to the State. At the time of the Massachusetts Constitutional Convention of 1820, John Adams tried to liberalize the "establishment" (which had been forced upon him in 1780); he moved to amend the clause on equal protection to provide for "all men of all religions" rather than "men of every denomination of Christians." [9] The amendment failed, but the whole system of public support of churches was defeated, in 1833, by a constitutional amendment which the voters ratified by a ten-to-one ratio. That was the end of the vestiges of theocracy, but not the end of arguments on its behalf. Orestes A. Brownson, after he was converted to Roman Catholicism, took up the Conservative theory.

Brownson, a man whose importance has been increasingly recognized, has not always been seen for what he was. One expects Arthur M. Schlesinger, Jr., to write better of Brownson's early radicalism than of his subsequent Conservatism, but even Catholics have tended to emphasize the democratic in Brownson and to ignore the antidemocratic,[10] to claim him as a defender of religious liberty and to forget his admiration for Fisher Ames and the ready acceptance his political ideas won from the most Conservative writer of his time, Tayler Lewis.[11]

The *Boston Quarterly Review,* which Brownson edited, was at first a platform for Liberal democracy. "Our rights and duties," wrote Brownson, "belong to us as men. . . . If all men have equal rights and duties . . . then is society bound to treat them as equals." [12] Like Emerson, Thoreau, Bancroft, and the Jacksonians of the *Democratic Review,* Brownson defended individual liberty against the power of the State: "Our danger is not from an excess of individuality, but from centralization. The danger to be apprehended is from the strength, not the weakness of the government." [13] Turning his attention to the problem of Church and State, Brownson—still a Unitarian—specifically rejected the argument that the United States was a Christian nation. He defended religious liberty in its most radical form: "If the Christian has the right, as a man, to defend his honest belief, the Deist, the Jew, the Atheist must have the same right." Laws compelling religious observances are "useless in the case of those who are religious, and can only produce hypocrisy in the case of those who are not." [14] Ministers err if they consider Christianity as "a curb, a bit, a restraint, a means by which the people may be kept in order. . . ." [15] In his often reprinted essay of 1840, "On the Labouring Classes," Brownson railed against "priestcraft" (by which he meant ministers of all churches): "The priest is universally a tyrant, universally the enslaver of his brethren, and therefore it is Christianity [which] condemns him." [16]

The Log-Cabin-and-Hard-Cider election of 1840 stunned Brownson. Harrison's victory shocked him so badly that he soon abandoned his magazine and started down the road to Catholic Conservatism.

> They who had devoted their lives to the cause of their country, of truth, justice, liberty, humanity, were looked upon as enemies of the people, and were unable to make themselves heard amid the maddened and maddening hurrahs of the drunken mob that went for "Tippecanoe, and Tyler too." [17]

The people were obviously incompetent to govern themselves: "This notion of theirs about self-government is all moonshine. . . ." [18] Brownson adopted a new slogan—"Liberty only in and through Order" [19]—and articulated a version of Conservatism importantly influenced by Joseph de Maistre: *

> We plant ourselves . . . on the firm reality of things, and content ourselves with gaining what can be gained with the means existing institutions furnish. We seek to advance religion through and in obedience to the Church; law and social well-being through and in obedience to the State.[20]

John L. O'Sullivan, editor of the *Democratic Review,* appended a disclaimer to each of Brownson's contributions and quickly terminated the agreement that had made Brownson a partner in the magazine.

Undeterred by O'Sullivan's displeasure, Brownson began to investigate the origins of government in order to locate the sources of authority. True to Catholic theory, he dismissed the idea that authority derives ultimately, by social contract or by any other means, from the people. "All power," he proclaimed in 1843, "is of God, and in the last analysis, no government is legitimate that

---

* Brownson drew upon de Maistre's *Essay on the Generative Principle of Political Constitutions,* which he reviewed at length in the October 1847 issue of *Brownson's Quarterly Review,* for the distinction between the "providential" constitution given by a nation's history and the artificial constitutions drawn up by feckless philosophers.

does not subsist by Divine Right." [21] Brownson stressed this conviction in a subsequent essay:

> The absolute and plenary sovereignty of God excludes all other sovereignty, and our absolute and unconditional subjection to him excludes all other subjection. Hence no liberty before God, and no subjection before man; and therefore liberty is rightly defined [as] full and entire freedom from all authority but the authority of God.[22]

Positive legislation contrary to divinely established natural law is *ipso facto* the invalid legislation of an illegitimate authority. To believe otherwise is to make the State absolute: "Unless . . . you exempt the state from all obligation even to the law of nature, you must make it amenable to the moral law as expounded by the Church, Divinely commissioned to teach and declare it." [23] When commanded by the State to violate natural law, the citizen must resist. Brownson answered the question asked of all theorists who make legitimacy the consequence of governmental adherence to natural law: who judges whether or not positive legislation is in accordance with natural law? Who decides whether or not resistance is justified? Brownson's answer was unequivocal: the Church decides; it belongs "to the Church . . . as the representative of the highest authority on earth, to determine when resistance is proper, and to prescribe its forms, and its extent. When this commands, it is our duty to obey." [24] (By "Church" Brownson meant, of course, the Roman Catholic Church, into which he was accepted October 20, 1844.) Father Stanley J. Parry, himself an acknowledged Conservative, is quite good on this aspect of Brownson's thought. In order to avoid the anarchy of individual judgment and the tyranny implied in the majoritarian's cry of *Vox populi, vox dei,* Brownson had to see the Church as arbiter of disputes over the legitimacy of legislation. In Parry's words, Brownson seeks

> a solution not in the ordinary providential order of history, not in the appeal of a purer natural knowledge of God's intention gained through abstract considerations, but rather . . .

in a new and supernatural movement of the Divine into the order of history—in Christ, that is to say, projected through history in his Mystical Body, the Church.[25]

This solution, continues Parry in truly Brownsonian phrases, "can be called authoritarian in the political sense only if one crudely thrusts upon [Brownson] a premise he never accepted: that the authority of the Church is a purely human authority." [26]

For these reasons, Brownson urged the "unity of Church and State" and condemned as inane the Liberal theory of separation of spheres. Although the Church was necessarily for the preservation of true liberty,[27] and ought logically to be established, Brownson recognized and made clear, especially in *The American Republic,* that legal establishment of Catholicism was both impractical and—in Brownson's optimistic view—unnecessary.

> The religious mission of the United States is not . . . to establish the church by external law, or to protect her by legal disabilities, pains, and penalties against the sects, however uncatholic they may be; but to maintain catholic freedom, neither absorbing the state in the church nor the church in the state, but leaving each to move freely . . . in the sphere assigned it in the eternal order of things. Their mission separates church and state as external governing bodies, but unites them in the interior principles from which each derives its vitality and force. Their union is in the intrinsic unity of principle, and in the fact that . . . each obeys one and the same Divine law.[28]

Which one of them interprets and the other enforces. The American mission is, then, to "harmonize" Church and State until the entire continent is comprised of "one grand nation, a really catholic nation, great, glorious, and free." [29]

2 *The Liberalization of the American Catholic Church*

Although Brownson's arguments were derived from medieval thought long familiar to theologians, the American hierarchy was distinctly embarrassed by Brownson's outspoken and belligerent statement of Catholic political theory.[30] The hierarchy preferred to stress the compatibility of Catholicism and democracy. Henry J. Browne exaggerates only slightly when he summarizes the history of the Catholic position of Church and State:

> The Catholic position as traditionally presented by theologians and canon lawyers holds that one true Church is to be recognized and treated as such by the state. The American . . . hierarchy, on the other hand, has constantly and consistently, from Carroll through Hughes and Gibbons up to Archbishop John McNicholas . . . of Cincinnati, and as late as 1948, expressed satisfaction with the American mode of separation, and evidenced no desire to change it, even should Catholics ever become an overwhelming majority of the population.[31]

The hierarchy's position was maintained *in spite of* the political encyclicals of Leo XIII. In order to understand the dilemma of the Church in America, one has to see just how far the American hierarchy departed from the Conservative traditions of the Church in their eager acceptance of the blessings of liberty.

The liberalization of American Catholicism, excellently studied by Robert D. Cross,[32] began with the Carroll family of Maryland. The Carrolls provided one signer of the Declaration of Independence, one signer of the Constitution, and the first great leader of the American Church. John Carroll, consecrated Bishop of Baltimore in 1790, was enthusiastic about the American relationship of Church and State. In an often quoted letter to the *Columbian Magazine,* he wrote:

> Thanks to genuine spirit and Christianity, the United States have banished intolerance from their system of government, and many of them have done the justice to every denomination of Christians, which ought to be done to them in all, of placing them on the same footing of citizenship, and conferring an equal right of participation in national privileges. Freedom and independence, acquired by the united efforts, and cemented with the mingled blood of Protestant and Catholic fellow-citizens, should be equally enjoyed by all. . . .[33]

Bishop Hughes of New York, Bishop Ireland of St. Paul, Bishop Spaulding of Peoria, and other members of the American hierarchy echoed Carroll's sentiments, but the most eloquent defender of the American way was probably Cardinal Gibbons. In the *North American Review,* this most important of nineteenth-century American clerics wrote:

> American Catholics rejoice in our separation of Church and State; and I can conceive [of] no combination of circumstances likely to arise which should make a union desirable either to Church or State. We know the blessings of our present arrangement; it gives us liberty and binds together priests and people in a union better than that of Church and State.[34]

Liberals within the Church today quote such statements proudly and often; they do not very frequently quote those bishops who opposed the liberalism of Ireland and Gibbons. One hears little of Archbishop Corrigan of New York, Bishop McQuaid of Rochester, and those clerics who rejoiced and felt themselves vindicated when Pius IX in 1864 specifically condemned the proposition that "The Church ought to be separated from the State and the State from the Church."[35] The fact of the matter is that Leo XIII, who followed Pius IX in 1878, formulated a Catholic theory of Church and State that was fundamentally incompatible with the American tradition of separation.

As Father John Courtney Murray and his supporters have patiently shown in a long series of scholarly books and articles, Leo XIII feared the anticlerical secularism of the European Liberal and did not fully understand the possibilities of a democratic society as it existed in the United States. But to understand the controversy within the Church, in the nineteenth century and in the twentieth, one must look briefly at Leo's response to the French Revolution and the revolutions that followed in its wake.

In the encyclical *Diuturnum* (1881), the first of the letters on political theory, Leo restated the traditional Catholic view of political authority. Authority derives from God and is conditional in the sense that civil authority never has the right to command "anything which violates the law of nature or the will of God."

Subsequent encyclicals, of which the seldom quoted *Immortale Dei* (1885) is the most important, made clear that the Church's role as judge of the legitimacy of authority necessitated the establishment of the Church. Because "rulers must bear in mind that God is the paramount ruler of the world, and must set Him before themselves as their exemplar and law in the administration of the State," there must be an orderly connection" between ecclesiastical and civil rulers. Separation of Church and State is, in principle, "wholly at variance with the truth." (In practice, Leo admitted that rulers had to preserve the peace of their realms and could not disturb the sanctions of custom. Separation was, in predominantly Protestant countries, an "article of peace.")

Immortale Dei was followed in 1888 by *Libertas Humana,* a forthright statement on religious liberty in a Catholic society:

> Justice . . . forbids, and reason itself forbids, the State to be godless; or to adopt a line of action which would end in godlessness—namely, to treat the various religions . . . alike, and to bestow upon them promiscuously equal rights and privileges. Since, then, the profession of one religion is necessary in the State, that religion must be professed which alone is true. . . .

In 1895, Leo turned his attention to the Church in the United States. The letter *Longinque Oceani* praises the American Church for its remarkable progress and American conditions for their contribution to that progress. Although the Church itself deserves the greater share of credit, "thanks are due to the equity of the laws which obtain in America and to the customs of the well-ordered Republic." Catholics anxious to refute the hysterical accusations of anticlericals ignore the qualifications that follow this praise of American conditions:

> Yet, though this be true, it would be very erroneous to draw the conclusion that in America is to be sought the type of the most desirable status of the Church, or that it would be universally lawful or expedient for State and Church to be, as in America, dissevered and divorced.

The Church would "bring forth more abundant fruits if, in addition to liberty, she enjoyed the favor of the laws and the patronage of the public authority."

Bishop Ireland was so upset by this statement that he cancelled an agreement to comment on the encyclical in the *North American Review*. Cardinal Gibbons, who was directly rebuked by Leo during the "Americanism" dispute of 1899,[36] learned to preface his praises of American life with the (seldom quoted) acknowledgment that "the most desirable relation" of Church and State in a predominantly Catholic country was "friendly union and co-operation." [37] But it was obvious to any reader or listener that Gibbons was far more enthusiastic about the practical than about the "ideal" arrangement.

The dispute within the Church, which reached one climax in the 1890's, has apparently reached another in the two decades since World War II. Father Francis J. Connell, one of the leaders of the Conservative wing of the Church, has consistently maintained that the twentieth-century pontiffs have been faithful to Leo's legacy and that the American Church cannot but heed their teachings. In one bellicose essay he quoted Pius XI's *Quas Primas* (1925) on the superiority of the ecclesiastical to the civil authority: "He would grievously err who would deny to Christ the government of all civil matters, since He receives from the Father the most absolute right over created things. . . ." Connell quoted Leo's *Immortale Dei* in his advocacy of governmental support of the only true Church, and he concluded, "We must unhesitatingly proclaim that the state cannot attain its destiny save through Christ the King. . . ." [38] The major challenge to this attempt to apply traditional doctrines to the contemporary situation has come from Father John Courtney Murray, who gradually developed in *Theological Studies* the argument that much of Catholic doctrine on politics is historically contingent and, for that reason, no longer relevant. Going back to Gelasius, Bellarmine, and John of Paris, Father Murray demonstrated that Leo's doctrine was applicable to the paternalistic society of the medieval period (and the nineteenth century in Europe) but inapplicable to the democratic societies of nineteenth-century America and twentieth-century Europe. Freedom of religion in a lay state was an "article of peace" that ought now become an "article of faith." Freedom of religion, in the ordinary rather than in the traditional Catholic sense, was not a necessary evil but a positive good.[39]

Father Murray was quickly engaged in debate by Father George W. Shea, who asserted that nothing had happened to change the truth of Leo's *Immortale Dei*.[40] Murray replied to Shea and was in turn sharply attacked by Father Joseph Fenton. The Church, growled Fenton, does not teach us to "understress any section of Catholic doctrine, simply because it happens to be unfashionable, or happens to be abused by anti-Catholic agitators at the time." [41] Even as Victor Yanitelli tried to chronicle the controversy, Fathers Murray and Connell continued to cut and slash their way through the pages of the *American Ecclesiastical Review*.[42] By the end of 1953, the Vatican itself was deeply involved. Alfredo Cardinal Ottaviani, Conservative Pro-Secretary of the Congregation of the Holy Office, quoted Father Murray (whom he did not name) and informed the liberals that *Immortale Dei* was still an authoritative document on Church and State.[43] Although Pius XII himself followed Ottaviani with milder statements, Father Murray was ordered by his Jesuit superiors to halt publication of his inflammatory theses on religious liberty.

The battle was lost but not the war. While Conservatives published their articles in theological journals read only by other clergy and often obtainable only at libraries of Catholic colleges, Fathers John Tracy Ellis, John Courtney Murray, Walter J. Ong, and Gustave Weigel have established themselves nationally as spokesmen respectfully attended by Protestants, Jews, and secularists, as well as Catholics. The liberals have on their side Jacques Maritain and Yves Simon, two internationally respected philosophers of Catholic democracy. The liberals have on their side a whole new generation of young historians, of whom

Michael Novak, Daniel Callahan, and John Ratté are representative, historians who rejoice in the end of the "Constantinian Era" and in the prospects of a free Church in an open society.

The liberals have on their side the first generation of sophisticated novelists to *remain* in the Church.* Harry Sylvester's novel, *Moon Gaffney,* is an attack on Catholic Conservatism; but it is also a bold affirmation of Catholic anarchism as found in Dorothy Day's Catholic-Worker movement. (The same movement which fostered the talents of Michael Harrington, author of *The Other America.*) J. F. Powers's brilliant comedy, *Morte d'Urban,* is a wildly funny account of a clerical operator who needles the liberals and bludgeons the Conservatives; the novel suggests that priests are human. The same suggestion can be found in William Michelfelder's *Be Not Angry,* an indictment of the "quicksands of rectory intrigue" and of the conspiratorial witlessness of Catholic-Action anticommunism, a defense of the clergy's commitment to the redemptive love that conquers all, even the creeds of the Church.

The liberals have on their side the Vatican itself. The most important change in the Church (as opposed to the Church in the United States) has undoubtedly been the change from Pius XII to John XXIII. Father Murray, silenced under Pius XII, was one of the chief actors at the Ecumenical Council which brought forth the epochal statement on religious liberty. Although Paul VI has evidenced, especially in his stand on birth control, a desire to make haste somewhat more slowly than his predecessor, there is little doubt that the American liberals have behind them what the Conservatives had in the nineteenth century—the authority of the Holy See. It is the turn of the Conservatives to protest against the Papacy's interference in the political realm.[44]

It is now at least possible that the American arrangement will

---

* American Catholicism, contrary to the usual allegations, has produced its share of first-rate writers. But Dreiser, Fitzgerald, Hemingway, O'Neill, O'Hara, Farrell, and McCarthy—to name a mixed handful—are scarcely to be considered as Catholic writers.

supersede the Spanish and the Portuguese as the ideal. Historians, political scientists, and sociologists can still point to a very high incidence of undemocratic attitudes and behavior among American Catholics; bigots are a hardy lot and will probably press their claims even in Utopia. But the signs of the times seem to point toward a continued democratization of Catholic theory and practice. The bases on which to construct a Conservative society continue slowly to erode.

3   T. S. Eliot's Homeward Voyage

Although American Catholicism in the twentieth century has produced no Conservative spokesman to rank with Orestes Brownson, America has produced a major figure to speak for the Conservative tradition of Church and State: T. S. Eliot, whom Russell Kirk correctly describes as a true successor to Burke and Coleridge. (The third edition of Kirk's *Conservative Mind* is subtitled *From Burke to Eliot.*)

Like Henry James, whose influence on his poetry is pervasive, Eliot had a sense of the past and a feel for the rich texture of European civilization. It was, in fact, precisely these traits to which he called attention in two essays on James, published in *The Little Review* in 1918.[45] The psychology of social existence was, in Eliot's sensitive estimate, the link between the art of Hawthorne and of James, the common bond of *The House of the Seven Gables* and *The Sense of the Past*. Eliot read these two books central to the Conservative tradition in America and felt the shock of recognition.

In his early poetry, especially in *The Waste Land* (1922), Eliot contrasted the fragmented and faithless modern world with the wholeness of earlier and allegedly happier times. Although irony qualifies almost every statement, the purposeless carnality of "the young man carbuncular" and the bored and tired typist seems distinctly inferior to the love celebrated in Spenser's poetry and Dante's. Echoes from the earlier poets sound through *The Waste*

Land and make contrast inevitable. Eliot sets Shakespeare's Anthony and Cleopatra, and St. Augustine's St. Augustine, off against

> Mr. Eugenides, the Smyrna merchant
> Unshaven, with a pocket full of currants
> C.i.f. London: documents in sight,
> Asked me in demotic French
> To luncheon at the Cannon Street Hotel
> Followed by a weekend at the Metropole.* [46]

Eliot pointed, in the early poems, to a world peopled by hollow men and by homeless men:

> My house is a decayed house,
> And the jew squats on the window sill, the owner,
> Spawned in some estaminet of Antwerp,
> Blistered in Brussels, patched and peeled in London.[47]

Even as Eliot displayed the shards of modern civilization, he began to develop a theory of literature compatible with Conservatism. In his most famous essay, "Tradition and the Individual Talent" (1919), Eliot depreciated the individualism which is the very center of Liberalism. The poet must "develop or procure the consciousness of the past"; he must extinguish his own personality: "What happens is a continual surrender of himself as he is at the moment to something which is more valuable. The progress of an artist is a continual self-sacrifice, a continual extinction of personality." [48] Literary tradition had, for Eliot, almost the prescriptive force the past has in Burke's philosophy. Technical innovation was justified because it enabled the poet better to preserve what seemed the very basis of civilization—Christianity.

In the decade that followed the publication of "Tradition and the Individual Talent," Eliot moved toward the explicit affirmation of Christianity in his poetry, toward "Ash-Wednesday,"

* From "The Waste Land," in T. S. Eliot, *Complete Poems and Plays*, reprinted by permission of Harcourt, Brace & World, Inc., and Faber and Faber Ltd.

Murder in the Cathedral and the first of the *Four Quartets* ("Burnt Norton"). In this same decade, Eliot realized that literary criticism was too narrow a field within which to work. "Literary criticism," he wrote, "should be completed by criticism from a definite ethical and theological standpoint." [49] His own standpoint was soon obvious. He announced himself, in the famous preface to *For Lancelot Andrewes* (1929), "classicist in literature, royalist in politics, and anglo-catholic in religion." In addition to essays on Anglican clergymen (Lancelot Andrewes, John Bramhall), the book contained "Niccolo Machiavelli," in which Eliot quoted the Italian on the social uses of an established church. In his cautious way, Eliot suggested agreement:

> It is quite possible that an established National Church, such as the Church of England, might have seemed to Machiavelli the best establishment for a Christian commonwealth; but that a religious establishment of some kind is necessary to a nation he is quite sure.[50]

In the Norton Lectures delivered at Harvard in 1932–33, Eliot dropped a remark, which he did not expand upon, that hints at the Conservative trend of his thoughts on Church and State: "To my mind, Racine's *Bérénice* represents about the summit of civilization in tragedy; and it is, in a way, a Christian tragedy, with devotion to the State substituted for devotion to divine law." [51] This substitution of Church for State is not an operation that anyone outside the Conservative tradition is likely to make.

Eliot turned in 1933, in his Page-Barbour lectures at the University of Virginia, to a detailed castigation of the strange gods of modern heresy. He had already, in his journal *Criterion,* warmly commended *I'll Take My Stand* (1930), the famous manifesto by twelve unreconstructed Southerners determined to defend their region against the urban, industrial, democratic, expansive society of the North.[52] In his lectures, Eliot hotly attacked modern civilization as "worm-eaten with Liberalism" [53] and repeated his commendation of the twelve Southerners. He added another support to his Conservative structure—religious homogeneity.

> The population [of a desirable society] should be homogeneous; where two or more cultures exist in the same place they are likely either to be fiercely self-conscious or both to become adulterate. What is still more important is unity of religious background; and reasons of race [sic] and religion combine to make any large number of free-thinking Jews undesirable. There must be a proper balance between urban and rural, industrial and agricultural development. And a spirit of excessive tolerance is to be deprecated.[54]

In his denunciation of the heretical D. H. Lawrence, Eliot slyly quoted from Pius IX's *Syllabus of Errors* (which he did not identify): "That we can and ought to reconcile ourselves to Liberalism, Progress and Modern Civilization is a proposition which we need not have waited for Lawrence to condemn; and it matters a good deal in what name we condemn it." [55] It matters, that is, that we condemn modern civilization in the name of Anglo-Catholicism rather than in the name of the Pope of Rome or, much worse, D. H. Lawrence's idiosyncratic version of Fascism.[56]

It was, however, Roman Catholicism toward which Eliot had moved in his consideration of the problem of Church and State. In *After Strange Gods,* he cited with approval Christopher Dawson, the most influential philosopher among English Catholic Conservatives in the 1930s. In several of the essays that appeared in *Criterion,* Eliot cited, again with approval, Joseph de Maistre (who had seldom been referred to by Americans since Orestes Brownson's laudatory references). Eliot chastized Sir Charles Petrie because his book in praise of monarchy lacked references to de Maistre and failed, therefore, fully to grasp the priority of ecclesiastical to civil authority. "Surely," complained Eliot, "the royalist can admit only one higher authority than the Throne, which is the Church." [57]

At the very time that Eliot wrote this rebuke of Petrie, he was

busy with a literary statement of de Maistre's principle of papal
supremacy—or, at least, with the argument that the Church represents an authority higher than the State. *Murder in the Cathedral,* his first and best play, vividly dramatizes the martyrdom,
in 1170, of Thomas Becket, Archbishop of Canterbury. Becket
had acted as King Henry's chancellor. Now, in opposition to the
secular authority, he rejects the temptation of temporal power: *

> No! shall I, who keep the keys
> Of heaven and hell, supreme alone in England,
> Who bind and loose, with power from the Pope,
> Descend to a punier power?
> Delegate to deal the doom of damnation,
> To condemn kings, not serve among their servants,
> Is my open office. . . .[58]

When King Henry's knights come with threats of death, Thomas
is adamant:

> It is not I who insult the King,
> And there is a higher than I or the King.
> It is not I, Becket from Cheapside,
> It is not against me, Becket, that you strive.
> It is not Becket who pronounces doom,
> But the Law of Christ's Church, the judgment of Rome.[59]

In a scene that Eliot never equaled for dramatic intensity, Thomas
is assassinated by the drunken knights (who then stand about
Becket in a circle, with swords pointed at the corpse, in physical
enactment of Eliot's favorite image of the turning wheel and its
still center). The knights attempt then anachronistically to rationalize their deed with the sophistries of twentieth-century secularism. (The anachronism shocks the spectator into the realiza-
tion that the whole meaning of the play is as relevant to the
present as the completely contemporary language of the rationali-

* From *Murder in the Cathedral,* in T. S. Eliot, *Complete Poems and Plays,*
reprinted by permission of Harcourt, Brace & World, Inc., and Faber and
Faber Ltd.

zations.) The play ends with a long chorus, the last lines of which are these:

> Lord, have mercy upon us.
> Christ, have mercy upon us.
> Lord, have mercy upon us.
> Blessed Thomas, pray for us.[60]

The Idea of a Christian Society, three lectures given at Corpus Christi College, Cambridge, completed the basic design. Although Eliot recognized that no society of our day can properly be termed "Christian," he feared—as he often repeated—that a civilization totally estranged from Christianity is impossible. One step toward a Christian society was surely the definition of the *idea* of one.

It is not necessary that all men be saints:

> The relation of the Christian State, the Christian Community, and the Community of Christians, may be looked at in connexion with the problem of *belief.* Among the men of state, you would have as a minimum, conscious conformity of behavior. In the Christian Community that they ruled, the Christian faith would be ingrained, but it requires, as a minimum, only a largely unconscious behavior; and it is only from the much smaller number of conscious human beings, the Community of Christians, that one would expect a conscious Christian life on its highest social level.[61]

The "lay state" of the secularists, and of such liberal Catholics as Father Murray, is rejected. The Christian organization of society is all but impossible without an established church. A "National Church" that forgets its connection with the "Universal Church" can be a great evil; nonetheless, the evils of disestablishment are greater: "I am convinced that you cannot have a national Christian society, a religious-social community, a society with a political philosophy founded upon the Christian faith, if it is constituted as a mere congeries of private and independent sects. The national faith must have an official recognition by the State, as well as an accepted status in the community and a basis of conviction in the heart of the individual." [62] The Church and State together will see to it that "the dissentients . . . remain marginal, tending to make only marginal contributions." [63]

Notes towards the Definition of Culture (1949) and *Of Poetry and Poets* (1957) add details to Eliot's model. In the former book, Eliot doubts that "the culture of Europe could survive the complete disappearance of the Christian Faith. . . . If Christianity goes, the whole of our culture goes." [64] He suggests also that society should be hierarchical, with a class based on inherited status as a necessary complement to an elite based on achievement. "What is important," he comments, "is a structure of society in which there will be, from 'top' to 'bottom,' a continuous gradation of cultural levels. . . ." This is not a defense of aristocracy; it is rather "a plea on behalf of a form of society in which an aristocracy should have a peculiar and essential function. . . ." [65] In his last major collection, *On Poetry and Poets,* Eliot was completely the sage. While somewhat more catholic in his poetic taste, he maintained his early commitment to the Jamesian sense of the past: "There is coming into existence," he warned, "a new kind of provincialism which perhaps deserves a new name. It is a provincialism, not of space, but of time; one for which history is merely the chronicle of human devices which have served their turn and been scrapped, one for which the world is the property solely of the living, a property in which the dead hold no shares." [66] His work, from first to last, is a *corpus* to which Conservatives may turn.

To this body of literature Russell Kirk does, indeed, urge Conservatives to turn.[67] He writes, "In the sixth decade of the twentieth century, Liberalism and socialism lie intellectually bankrupt, and for the most part fallen from . . . favor. If Conservatively inclined men of affairs can rise to the summons of the poets, the norms of culture and politics may endure in defiance of the crimes and follies of the age." [68] Since Kirk wrote these brave words, the American people have elected a Catholic President whose interpretation of the proper relation of Church and State would have been the despair of Leo XIII and a Protestant President whose passion seems to be for egalitarianism at home and dominion abroad. Neither man is admired by Conservatives.

It is perhaps a measure of the decline of American Conservatism that the only major twentieth-century champion of its theory of Church and State boarded ship, like the Tories of the 1770's, and sailed off to become a British subject. He returned —in his poetry—to "Gerontion's" image of the decayed house. "East Coker," the second of the *Four Quartets,* begins:

> In my beginning is my end. In succession
> Houses rise and fall, crumble, are extended,
> Are removed, destroyed, restored, or in their place
> Is an open field, or a factory, or a by-pass.
> Old stone to new building, old timber to new fires,
> Old fires to ashes, and ashes to the earth
> Which is already flesh, fur and faeces,
> Bone of man and beast, cornstalk and leaf.
> Houses live and die: there is a time for building
> And a time for living and for generation
> And a time for the wind to break the loosened pane
> And to shake the wainscot where the field-mouse trots
> And to shake the tattered arras woven with a silent motto.*

Like Clifford Pyncheon and Ralph Pendrel, Eliot journeyed home. He wrote in "East Coker" of his family's origins: "Home is where one starts from." But home was England, and not America. Eliot is buried now in Somerset, in the place from which his seventeenth-century ancestors set forth for the New World. His career is an emblem of the estrangement of American Conservatism from the predominantly secular and democratic course of the American Republic.

* From "East Coker," in *Four Quartets,* copyright © 1943, by T. S. Eliot. Reprinted by permission of Harcourt, Brace & World, Inc., and Faber and Faber Ltd.

IV

Conservatism and the Military Establishment *

1 The Military Ethic and the Literary Mind

Political and economic power unprecedented in history are now concentrated at the Pentagon. The military establishment takes more than 50 per cent of the Federal budget, more than 10 per cent of the Gross National Product. The biological and thermo-nuclear weapons at its disposal awe the leaders of this nation even as they deter (we hope) the leaders of the communist bloc. Although total war seems unlikely, limited wars are and will probably continue to be fought. The Test-Ban Treaty of 1963 was an important step toward a *détente* between the United States and the Soviet Union, but effective disarmament supervised by an adequately empowered United Nations remains a visionary prospect.

Long before the raids to the North that signaled increased American involvement in Vietnam, Americans upset by the danger inherent in concentrated power denounced "militarism," "the military mind," "the Warfare State," the "war hawks of Washington," and the "nuclear witch doctors." The Department

---

* An earlier version of this chapter appeared as "Political Ideals and the Military Ethic," *American Scholar*, XXXIV (1965), 221–37.

of Defense has been condemned for its alleged commitment to the "Prussianized military-industrial concept . . . that produced Hitler." Recent history has been mythologized: "The ultra-conservative classes that rule our 'military-industrial complex' and dominate our society have led us into an age of social upheaval and revolution, obsessed by a paranoid phobia of change and revolution." [1] The myth is not entirely unrelated to reality, but it obscures as much as it reveals. The professional soldier cannot be understood if he is labeled "authoritarian" and told to stand in a corner.

Samuel Huntington's very important book, *The Soldier and the State,* demonstrates that the abusive attacks on "nuclear militarism" derive from the "confused and unsystematic . . . assumptions and beliefs" of American Liberalism.* [2] Preliminary to constructing an alternative framework within which to analyze the military ethic and the problem of civil-military relations, Huntington knocks to pieces the traditional Liberal model:

> The heart of Liberalism is individualism. It emphasizes the reason and moral dignity of the individual, and opposes political, economic, and social restraints upon individual liberty. In contrast, the military ethic holds that man is evil, weak, and irrational and that he must be subordinated to the group. The military man claims that the natural relation among men is conflict. . . . [3]

The Liberal fears power and believes in peace through international law. The Liberal is antimilitary because the army *is* the State as coercive power in its most concentrated form. To be suspicious of the State is to be fearful of the army, the State in its ultimate and—for the Liberal—least attractive form. Readers unconvinced by Huntington's account of the military establishment can turn to Arthur A. Ekirch's avowedly Liberal and antimilitary book, *The Civilian and the Military.* Ekirch documents fully the

---

* The material quoted in this chapter from Samuel P. Huntington, *The Soldier and the State,* is reprinted by permission of The Belknap Press of Harvard University Press.

long American struggle to do without a professional army—and, characteristically, admonishes us to beware the loss of liberty to the "Garrison State" (the phrase is Harold Lasswell's).[4]

What political theory, according to Huntington, is implicit in the military ethic? Conservatism. Like the Conservatism of Edmund Burke, whom Huntington cites in order explicitly to dismiss the nineteenth-century Liberalism that passes as "conservatism" in popular parlance, the military ethic "stresses the supremacy of society over the individual and the importance of order, hierarchy, and division of function. It stresses the continuity and value of history."[5] The soldier is the antithesis of the businessman. He seeks honor under a military code which, in Douglas MacArthur's words, "has come down to us from even before the age of knighthood and chivalry." He is contemptuous of commercialism, aloof from partisan politics and skeptical of the attempt to "outlaw" war as a means of settling international disputes. "The military ethic," writes Huntington, "is basically corporative in spirit." It is hierarchical. "It is fundamentally anti-individualistic."[6]

Corroboration of Huntington's theses is to be had in the literature of World Wars I and II. There is at hand, or in the library, an immense stack of fiction. Although the message of most of the popular novels is bellicose (Hang the Kaiser! Remember Pearl Harbor!), the best novels, which are the ones mentioned in most discussions of the literary response to war, are written from a Liberal perspective. They are antimilitary.

In *Three Soldiers* and *Soldier's Pay,* John Dos Passos and William Faulkner wrote bitterly of a generation lost to Mars. E. E. Cummings was more even-tempered in *The Enormous Room,* but Ernest Hemingway's stories and novels of World War I are filled with men physically and spiritually wounded, men whose only hope was for a separate peace. The tradition has been carried on by Norman Mailer, Hemingway's great disciple, rival, admirer, and critic. In the complex fictive world of *The Naked and the Dead,* one finds the Liberal's (or the Marxist's) archetype of the professional soldier, a general with homosexual tendencies who believes in the "concept of fascism, far sounder than communism if you consider it, for it's grounded firmly in men's actual natures, merely started in the wrong country, in a country which did not have enough intrinsic potential power to develop completely."

Noting that Mailer's novel "falls squarely within the great American tradition of antiwar, antimilitary literature," [7] Huntington turns, in *The Soldier and the State,* to Herman Wouk's best seller, *The Caine Mutiny*. The novel is essentially Conservative. Although authority, as embodied in Captain Queeg, is morally defective and professionally incompetent, it is authority nonetheless, and ought to be obeyed. Queeg was an officer of the Navy that defended us all when most of us pursued our private pleasures. In Huntington's paraphrase, "The real hero is none of the individual figures, but the United States Navy itself. The junior officers of the *Caine* should have served in silence under Queeg because he was part of the system, and the disruption of the system does more harm than the suffering of individual injustice." [8] The villain of the book is the Liberal intellectual who fails to comprehend the moral truth suggested by the very name of the ship.

The most impressive literary corroboration of Huntington's thesis is not, however, *The Caine Mutiny,* a book which reduces the moral dilemma to comic-book dimensions. The Conservative implications of the military ethic are most powerfully dramatized in an earlier work, Herman Melville's *Billy Budd*.

The political context of Melville's story is specified. The first page contains allusions to the French Revolution. The relationships are made explicit in the third chapter: "It was the summer of 1797. In the April of that year had occurred the commotion at Spithead followed in May by a second and yet more serious outbreak in the fleet at the Nore." The men of the British navy had mutinied. "Reasonable discontent growing out of practical grievances in the fleet had been ignited into irrational combustion as by live cinders blown across the Channel from France in flames." Billy Budd is, moreover, impressed from a ship named *Rights-of-Man* by an owner who was "a staunch admirer of Thomas Paine, whose book is rejoinder to Burke's arraignment of the French Revolution had then been published for some time and had gone everywhere." His "natural right" to mutiny was greater than that of the bluejackets who had enlisted in the navy.

Melville emphasizes the goodness of Billy Budd, and the malignity of Claggart, Billy's antagonist, by repeated allusions to Adam before the Fall and to "the arch interferer, the envious marplot of Eden." (He also likens Billy to the gods and heroes of Greece.) He strongly emphasizes the Conservatism of Captain Vere, the ship's commander:

> [Vere's] settled convictions were as a dike against those invading waters of novel opinion, social, political, and otherwise, which carried away as in a torrent no few minds in those days, minds by nature not inferior to his own. While other members of that aristocracy to which by birth he belonged were incensed at the innovators mainly because their theories were inimical to the privileged classes, Captain Vere disinterestedly opposed them not alone because they seemed to him insusceptible of embodiment in lasting institutions, but at war with the peace of the world and the true welfare of mankind.

Vere is, in effect, a disciple of Edmund Burke.

The crisis comes when Billy, falsely accused of plotting mutiny, stammers and is unable to speak. He strikes and kills his accuser. Vere's instant judgment contains the central paradox of the book: "Struck dead by an angel of God! Yet the angel must hang!" Although Vere knows Billy to be innocent in the eyes of God, innocent under Nature's law, he also recognizes that Billy lives in society and has committed a crime for which he must pay. Where Captain Queeg was inarticulate, paranoid, and totally unpersuasive, Vere is heroic. He puts the dilemma to the court-martial:

How can we adjudge to summary and shameful death a fellow creature innocent before God, and whom we feel to be so?—Does that state it aright? You sign sad assent. Well, I too feel that, the full force of that. It is Nature. But do these buttons that we wear attest that our allegiance is to Nature? No, to the King. Though the ocean, which is inviolate Nature primeval, though this be the element where we move and have our being as sailors, yet as the King's officers lies our duty in a sphere correspondingly natural? So little is that true, that in receiving our commissions we in the most important regards ceased to be natural free agents. When war is declared are we the commissioned fighters previously consulted? We fight at command.

Vere is interrupted by an officer of marines who argues that "Budd proposed neither mutiny nor homicide." Vere answers, "Surely not, my good man. And before a court less arbitrary and more merciful than a martial one, that plea would largely extenuate. At the Last Assizes it shall acquit. But how here? We proceed under the law of the Mutiny Act." And the Mutiny Act calls for Billy to be hanged.

Vere's Conservatism is undeniable, but Melville's is doubtful. The question of Melville's own acceptance of Vere's views has agitated many critics and is not likely to be settled here.[9] The execution scene itself is filled with ambiguities. Billy's last words are, "God bless Captain Vere!" With the hemp around his neck, he seems like Christ on the cross, an association that Melville's imagery makes unmistakable. Vere himself is killed in combat against the ship *St. Louis,* renamed the *Athée,* and he dies with Billy's name on his lips. The story ends with Billy a legend, with a ballad, "Billy in the Darbies [handcuffs]."

> . . . me they'll lash in hammock, drop me deep.
> Fathoms down, fathoms down, how I'll dream fast asleep.
> I feel it stealing now. Sentry, are you there?
> Just ease these darbies at the wrist,

> And roll me over fair!
> I am sleepy, and the oozy weeds about me twist.

It seems probable that Melville was at least as committed to the dream of innocence, to the American Adam, as to Conservatism's pessimistic credo. Fortunately, we need not decide, for our present purposes, whether *Billy Budd* is Melville's final affirmation of innocence or his "testament of acceptance." [10] It is enough to see that Vere's ship, the H.M.S. *Bellipotent,* is a microcosm of society itself and that Vere is the essential Conservative, the personification of the military ethic that Huntington has described.

Literary corroboration is not, however, proof. The novelist, despite the extravagant claims of Émile Zola, presents an inherently unscientific and unverifiable vision of reality. The novelist projects attitudes rather than facts; he creates in imagination another world that is a judgment of the ordinary world rather than a description of it. The great novelist misleads those who take his metaphors as literal statements. The rigorous arguments of *The Soldier and the State* end in a curious two-page symbolic opposition of the "ordered serenity" of West Point and the "incredible variety and discordancy of small-town commercialism":

> The post is suffused with the rhythm and harmony which comes when collective will supplants individual whim. West Point is a community of structured purpose, one in which the behavior of men is governed by a code, the product of generations. There is little room for presumption and individualism. . . . In order is found peace; in discipline, fulfillment; in community, security. . . . The spirit of West Point is in the great, gray, Gothic Chapel, starting from the hill and dominating The Plain, calling to mind Henry Adams' remarks at Mont St. Michel on the unity of the military and the religious spirits. But the unity of the Chapel is even greater. There join together the four great pillars of society: Army, Government, College, and Church. Religion subordinates man to God for divine purposes; the military life subordinates man to duty for society's purposes. In its severity, regularity, discipline, the

military society shares the characteristics of the religious order. Modern man may well find his monastery in the Army.[11]

Is it possible that *The Soldier and the State* contains, along with much brilliant historical and sociological analysis, a passionate projection of attitudes, a model of the military ethic that is an almost literary construct, a portrait similar to Melville's because painted by imagination's lamp? Is it also possible that some third polity fits the military ethic better than Liberalism or Conservatism? It is possible. The implicit—but certainly not the explicit— polity of the American military establishment today is a pragmatic form of social democracy usually described, in popular speech, as "modern Liberalism."

2 Liberalism, Socialism, and the American Soldier

Addressing the Corps of Cadets at West Point, Douglas MacArthur made his (and West Point's) credo the refrain of his speech:

> Duty-Honor-Country. Those three hallowed words reverently dictate what you ought to be, what you can be, what you will be. They are your rallying points. . . . You are the leaven which binds together the entire fabric of our national system of defense. From your ranks come the great captains who hold the nation's destiny in their hands the moment the war tocsin sounds. The Long Gray Line has never failed us. Were you to do so, a million ghosts in olive drab, in brown khaki, in blue and gray, would rise from their white crosses, thundering those magic words—Duty-Honor-Country.[12]

Insofar as the soldier remains loyal to these ideals he continues in the Conservative tradition; he opposes the capitalistic code of individual profit best epitomized in the Robber Baron's epigram: "Nothing is lost save honor!"

How typical is MacArthur? Not very. The memoirs of Ulysses S. Grant and William T. Sherman are remarkable for their plain style and their understated descriptions of the movements of troops. Although Southerners came closer to the European ideal of honor than did Northerners, American soldiers—except for MacArthur—have seldom written or behaved in a manner Charles de Gaulle might think properly military. And, as Morris Janowitz notes in his excellent *The Professional Soldier,* honor has become less and less significant in our military establishment as the "heroic leaders" are replaced by the "military managers." [13] Pierre Gustave Toutant de Beauregard strutted Napoleonically, but Stonewall Jackson was the future's voice when he told his men to shoot rather than cheer the courageous enemy; the brave ones spurred the others on.

The leaders of World War II were remarkably unsympathetic to the aristocratic codes of enemy and ally. General Wainwright objected to the Japanese soldier's "foggy, medieval" beliefs; the banzai charge and "ritualistic hari-kari" were not the "tactics of reason." [14] General Stilwell answered bitterly the British scorn for "unmilitary" Americans. His diary references to British officers are closer in tone to Mark Twain than to MacArthur. Sir Harold Alexander is, for instance, "astonished to find ME—mere me, a goddam American—in command of Chinese troops. 'Extrawdinary!' Looked me over as if I had just crawled out from under a rock." [15] General Chennault, in the same China-Burma-India theater, scorned the inefficient traditionalism of the British and boasted of his slovenly but effective Flying Tigers. In France, homespun Omar Bradley and roughneck George Patton (with less justice) objected loudly to the theatrics and the ambitions of General Montgomery.

It was, however, the French concept of military honor that most bewildered the American soldier. Before the North African invasion, Robert Murphy, career diplomat, had to explain carefully to Eisenhower that the French officers took their oaths of allegiance to Pétain very seriously. Eisenhower's own account of the attempt to win Darlan from Vichy is a study in incomprehension. General Patton, described by his latest biographer as "a medieval personality," was astonished when told that the "friendly" resistance of General Noguès's Moroccan forces enabled the French partially to recoup honor lost in the terrible *Blitzkrieg*.[16] General Truscott's attitude breaks through his quotation marks: "It was expected that the French would resist any assault landing in Morocco, but it was hoped it would be a token resistance, sufficient only to satisfy the demands of 'French honor.'"[17] Ironic quotation marks punctuate Ladislas Farago's account of Patton's troubles with Admiral Michelier; General Clark uses quotation marks against Darlan, Giraud, and Juin: "I was unhappy at the way I was . . . forced to bluster and push people around, and I was irritated by the fog of French personal and political 'honor' that seemed to be holding up our military plans."[18] In contrast to MacArthur's religious imagery ("Rally to me. . . . The guidance of Divine God points the way. Follow in His name to the Holy Grail of righteous victory!"), General Clark's metaphors are commercial: "Darlan was a political investment forced upon us by circumstances, but we made a sensational profit in lives and time through using him."[19] Men fought and died because there was a job to be done and they were trained to do it. There were few *chevaliers sans peur et sans reproche* among the generals and admirals of World War II.

Compared to the American businessman, the soldier is the personification of ceremony and tradition. Compared to the European soldier, the American is as deficient in reverence for the past as in a sense of military honor. The study of history is a part of military education and West Point has its sense of the past, but the American soldier has from the first been schooled in engineering (or navigation) rather than in history. The professional *uses* rather than reveres the past and prides himself not as the inheritor and preserver but as the innovator and improviser. Military leaders have, like men in business, government, education, the ministry, resisted change. Patton wept at the end of the cavalry—and was our greatest tank commander. Resistance comes harder and harder. In an age when obsolescence overtakes a weapons system on the drawing board, at a time when civilians like Brodie, Kahn, Kissinger, and Morgenstern debate the problems of strategy, military leadership is more often exercised by the "military intellectuals" (like James M. Gavin) than by officers sensitive to traditional ways. Lee's lieutenants might still have had a Burkean sense of the prescriptive power of inherited custom; McNamara's lieutenants do not.

A code of honor and a sense of history are one side of the coin; the other side, which Huntington emphasizes, is a rejection of capitalistic economics, partisan politics, and pacifistic foreign policy. Although Huntington quotes impressively from professional journals' attacks on commercialism which demonstrate "a thoroughly noneconomic conservatism," [20] his generalizations seem better suited to European society, where the antagonism between soldier and businessman is an old tradition. Consider William T. Sherman, whom Huntington cites as *the* professional soldier (in contrast to the utterly unsatisfactory Ulysses S. Grant). Sherman's memoirs show little sense of the importance of honor and a great awareness of commercial possibilities. While on active duty in California, he went into the grocery business. While stationed in St. Louis, he speculated in realty. Like Grant and many other West Pointers of this period, he resigned from the Army and went into business. For most of the decade before 1861 he was a banker in San Francisco and New York. Consider Douglas MacArthur himself. Even in his West Point address, he paused to denounce "deficit financing" and high taxes. After dismissal from command, he toured the nation and urged the preservation of laissez-faire capitalism: "There are those who seek to change our system of free enterprise which, whatever its faults, commands the maximum energy from human resource and provides maximum benefits in human happiness. . . ." [21] Neither Morris Janowitz nor Richard Brown (who studied the social attitudes of 465 generals from 1898 to 1940) finds serious antagonism to private-enterprise capitalism. On the contrary, the average soldier is convinced that private enterprise is the *sine qua non* of the

American Way. This conviction can be seen in the postretirement employment of hundreds of general and flag officers (including MacArthur) with major corporations engaged in military procurement. As the attacks on the "power elite" and "the warfare state" invariably demonstrate, movement from the Pentagon to Wall Street is rather easy.

And what of politics? Huntington points to Sherman's refusal to run if nominated or serve if elected as *the* symbol of the apolitical tradition of the professional soldier. It is still true that Taylor, Grant, and Eisenhower ran successfully for the presidency, Winfield Scott, George McClellan, and Winfield Scott Hancock ran unsuccessfully, and Leonard Wood, George Dewey, and Douglas MacArthur wanted to run. One can make a case for the apolitical military elite only if one insists that Sherman, Pershing, and Ridgway exemplify the professional while the others do not. The involvement of the military in politics has, as Huntington himself brilliantly shows in *The Common Defense,* grown steadily greater, not because we have moved toward a "Garrison State" but because the determination of military policy is *"always* the product of politics" and now perhaps the single most important question of American politics.[22]

Huntington is unquestionably right on one important point. The military ethic's recognition of the role of power is Conservative rather than Liberal. The professional soldier is by Harold Lasswell's definition a "specialist in violence." He steps in when the rule of law has failed. The contrast between the militarist and the pacifist is almost total; General H. Wager Halleck could not begin his famous *Elements of Military Art and Science* (1846) without a lengthy rebuttal of Francis Wayland's popular essays on behalf of pacifism. (Wayland was also, of course, an apostle of laissez-faire.) Through the 1890's Alfred Thayer Mahan's books on sea power answered (indirectly) Andrew Carnegie and other exemplars of "business pacifism."

But the Liberal too goes to war. Because he totally rejects the Clausewitzian dicta about the continuum of war and peace, he

fights to end an unnatural situation (war) and to restore a natural one (peace). Surrender must be unconditional so that the
warmongers can be permanently pacified. In the ironic paraphrase of Raymond Aron, "The enemy was guilty and deserved
punishment, was wicked and must be corrected. Afterward, peace
would prevail." [23]

To a remarkable extent, this attitude has been accepted by the
professional soldier. Writing to General Halleck from captured
Atlanta, Sherman insisted, "If the people raise a howl against my
barbarity and cruelty, I will answer that war is war, and not
popularity-seeking. If they want peace, they and their relatives
must stop the war." [24] Writing from France in World War I,
Pershing displayed the same attitude: "Complete victory can only
be obtained by continuing the war until we force unconditional
surrender from Germany; but if the Allied Governments decide
to grant an armistice, the terms should be so rigid that under no
circumstances could Germany again take up arms." [25] The same
attitude led to the use of nuclear weapons against Japan and the
subsequent disavowal of war in the Japanese constitution.

Because peace is peace and war is war, political considerations
play no part in wartime. Therefore, Eisenhower saw neither the
significance of the differences between Admiral Darlan and General de Gaulle nor the importance of American capture of Berlin
and Prague (which an element of Patton's Third Army entered
four days before the Russians). As Bradley commented in *A Soldier's Story,* "At times during that war, we forgot that wars are
fought for the resolution of political conflicts. . . ." [26] MacArthur,
unable to comprehend the Clausewitzian doctrine of limited war,
provided a Liberal slogan to equal "unconditional surrender":
"There is no substitute for victory." [27] Meanwhile, civilians anxious to construct a theory of foreign policy free from the "legalist
and moralistic" errors of Liberalism have become the apostles of
a "realistic" theory of international relations, a theory based on
the recognition of the role of power in foreign affairs. [28]

In these trying times of controversy over American intervention in Vietnam, a further word must be added *à propos* the military view of power. The Pentagon certainly tends to urge military rather than diplomatic solutions to the problems of foreign policy, but the stereotype of *Dr. Strangelove,* with its mad general unleashing nuclear bombers, is slapstick, not comedy; comedy amuses *and* enlightens. A military establishment that did *not* seek in the middle of a war, even a limited war, to defeat the enemy in battle would betray the nation it was supposed to defend. It is for civilian authority, for the President and his advisors in and out of Congress, to determine when military efforts should be supplemented and finally supplanted by political and economic efforts. The available evidence indicates that it was Woodrow Wilson who decided to take up the German challenge in 1917, that it was Franklin Roosevelt who felt long before Pearl Harbor that the time had come to quarantine the aggressors, that it was Harry S Truman who committed an American army to the defense of Korea, that it was Dwight D. Eisenhower, John F. Kennedy, and Lyndon B. Johnson who put Americans into Vietnam.

The truth is that the foreign policy of great powers, whether democratic or undemocratic in their domestic social organization, has always been fundamentally different from the foreign policy of minor powers. There is an immense contrast between a foreign policy democratically arrived at and a democratic foreign policy. Thucydides understood this. Using the words of the Athenians and not the Spartans, he wrote: "The powerful exact what they can and the weak grant what they must." [29] Sociology is more sober: "The number of wars in which a nation participates measures the role played by each state on the international stage rather than the aggressiveness of the state or the people involved." [30] This observation by Raymond Aron follows a discussion of Quincy Wright's enormous tome, *A Study of War,* in which Wright shows that England, in the years 1480–1941, fought more wars than any other nation. John Adams, in a note scribbled in the margin of a book, came to the same unhappy conclusion: "England the free has not been less disposed to war than France,

Spain, Germany, Prussia, and Russia the despotic." [31] It is naïve to explain a powerful nation's aggressive pursuit of what it deems its national interest by references to the mentality of generals and admirals. The problem is more serious, and one of the gravest dangers is that policy-makers will give way to the Liberal public's clamor for an immediate solution to international ills. It is certainly not helpful to be advised to bomb the rest of mankind back to the Stone Age in order to retire to the peaceful ramparts of Fortress America. It is no more helpful to be told to make love and not war.

One must admit that, however much the American soldier may depart from the Conservative model in other respects, the ideal of military discipline is basically contradictory to the Jeffersonian tradition of individual rights and the Emersonian glorification of self-reliance. The American military allows its officers and men a freedom of action—off-duty and in combat—unknown in European armies.* But the freedom has its obvious limits. Military discipline, defined by the *Officer's Guide,* "rests upon the voluntary subordination of the individual to the welfare of the group." In an age of total war and the Selective Service Act, the adjective "voluntary" is a gesture. The soldier may be, if he likes, a reader of *Walden* and "Civil Disobedience." When commanded to move across a field in the face of enemy fire, he moves. In MacArthur's words, "In many businesses and professions the welfare of the individual is the chief object, but in the military profession the safety and honor of the state becomes paramount." [32] Individual liberty, as Burke argued, must be subordinated when necessary to the needs of the society that makes liberty possible in the first place.

Burke's Conservatism and military organization are, moreover, both hierarchical. But the hierarchy of army and navy is not that

---

* A remarkable instance of this freedom occurred in 1946 when, in the wake of victory over Germany and Japan, military discipline collapsed. See R. Alton Lee, "The Army 'Mutiny' of 1946," *Journal of American History,* LIII (1966), 555–71.

of Conservative society. Once again, the military ethic departs from the Conservative course. Status in the military establishment derives from rationally defined *function* and not from hereditary membership in a social class. The military commonplace—"Salute the rank and not the man"—is an apt vernacular translation of Robert K. Merton's definition of bureaucratic authority: "Authority, the power of control which derives from an acknowledged status, inheres in the office and not in the particular person who performs the official role." [33] Neither birth nor wealth is a factor in military leadership—except to the degree that accidents of birth enable some more readily than others to acquire the skills and to demonstrate the qualities that are a prerequisite to advancement. To achieve its present degree of professionalization, the European army repudiated the nobility's "right" to military leadership; to achieve *its* professionalization, the American military had to prevent appointment to high rank of civilians with political influence. The success of the army can be seen in the failure of Senator McCarthy to attain for Private G. David Schine anything like the military position won by politically influential civilians in the Civil War.

In short, the professional soldier in America departs markedly from the Conservative model. No important soldier has expressed his commitment to Russell Kirk's program for a truly Burkean society, and it is unlikely that any will. These generalizations are essentially negative, but they suggest the positive: the professional soldier shares rather than opposes the Liberal democratic tradition that dominated American life from (at the very least) the collapse of the Federalist party to the coming of the New Deal.

Although military men in their professional journals have sometimes expressed hostility to the processes of democracy, the military elite in its postwar pinnacle of power has adhered closely to the traditional rhetoric. MacArthur's *Reminiscences* are threaded through with the general's professions of his devotion to liberty and to the dignity of the individual. Eisenhower's *Crusade in Europe* concludes with a defense of liberal democracy. "Individual liberty," writes the general, "rooted in human dignity, is man's greatest treasure." [34] Eisenhower as President thrilled millions (and bored other millions) with endless eulogies to peace and progress, individual liberty, and equal rights. James M. Gavin declares himself for "our democratic system which stems from a way of life that encourages the individual to develop himself as fully as his God-given talents will allow. . . ." [35] Matthew Ridgway, the soldier's soldier, opposed officers who wasted lives for "glory" with the argument that "all lives are equal on the battlefield. . . . The dignity which attaches to the individual is the basis of Western civilization." [36] From Omar Bradley, Mark Clark, Lucius Clay, George C. Marshall, William Westmoreland, and a score of others one could compile an anthology of similar declarations.

Do they mean what they say? Members of the Communist party and of the John Birch Society might well agree that Eisenhower and Marshall acted undemocratically from ignorance or guile, but most of us are ready to admit at least the good intentions of these men even as we see that their political actions took them far to the Left of such prominent civilians as Senators Knowland, Jenner, McCarthy, Taft, Byrd, Eastland, McCarran, and Thurmond. It was West Point-educated Eisenhower whose mania for a balanced budget drove generals into despair and retirement; it was Harvard-educated Kennedy who heeded the strategists in their appeals for a deterrent system composed of conventional and nuclear weapons, limited war capability in addition to the first-strike and second-strike weapons of massive retaliation. It was the Ivy Leaguers in the C.I.A. and not the graduates of Annapolis and West Point who subverted the Arbenz government in Guatemala and the neutralist coalition in Laos, who overthrew Mossadegh in Iran and managed the fiasco at the Bay of Pigs.

The sincerity of the generals' professions of democratic faith can be tested in their careers as proconsuls in postwar Germany and Japan. Lucius Clay, often in advance of civilian advisors, worked with skill and dedication to construct what may be—for all its imperfections—the first stable democracy in German history. Patton, who never understood why Americans fought, was quickly relieved of all responsibility. MacArthur's career as the Emperor's temporary replacement won the reluctant praises even of Richard Rovere and Arthur M. Schlesinger, Jr., two of his most articulate dispraisers. The worst blot on his reputation in Japan, his harsh suppression of communist activities, is less black than congressional legislation depriving the C.P.U.S.A., far weaker than its Japanese counterpart, of political rights.

It cannot be denied that many retired generals and admirals have allied themselves with the Radical Right. But these men are politically Liberal in their anachronistic commitment to laissez-faire economics (jeopardized by the New Deal and perfidious Income Tax) and in their unshaken faith in an anticommunist foreign policy that assumes war and peace to be, like good and evil, separate and distinct. These men are, in addition, dispossessed even within the military. Bonner Fellers, George Stratemeyer, James Van Fleet, Albert C. Wedemeyer, and Charles A. Willoughby are all "Far Easterners" who served with MacArthur, all men displaced from the dominant line of Marshall, Eisenhower, Bradley, Ridgway, Taylor, and Lemnitzer. They are also the men displaced by civilian theorists and by the military managers who have accepted the strategic implications of modern technology. "The primary appeal of the Radical Right," comments Huntington, "has been to the older officers, retired from the military hierarchy and unfamiliar with and hostile to the new expertise." [37] They are angry and bewildered men who have joined as followers, not as leaders, Barry Goldwater and Billy James Hargis and others who do not see why "normalcy" could not have returned after World War II. Undoubtedly, there are men on the Right who have dreamed of the Man on Horseback, the heroic leader who can rally "true" Americans in a *Kulturkampf* against alien ideas. Undoubtedly, there are officers who would like to play the role. But they have not acted, and it seems unlikely that they will. Meanwhile, most of the officer corps, like the majority of civilians, accept the social reforms of the past thirty years, articulate the no longer applicable rhetoric of nineteenth-century Liberalism, and go about their business. "The political beliefs of the military," writes Janowitz, "are not distinct from those that operate in civilian society." *

The conviction lingers that the soldier must be different from the civilian. *The American Soldier,* the two-volume report by Samuel Stouffer and others employed by the army in World War II, begins with the stereotyped Liberal description of the army as traditionalist, authoritarian, "highly stratified," with "hierarchies of deference . . . formally and minutely established by official regulation." [38] But the evidence that follows, for a thousand pages, does not support the initial assertions. [39] The data show officers and enlisted men to be remarkably alike in their attitudes on every subject except, understandably, their relations to each other. Soldiers differ little in attitude from civilians with similar racial, economic, educational, or geographical background.

The disparity between the sociologists' *a priori* assumptions and the empirical data can be clearly seen in the professional journals. Descriptions of the army as hierarchical, rigidly stratified, "caste-like," feudalistic, and dominated by "the medieval tradition," are followed—after a lapse of several years—by puzzled articles in which elaborate tests indicate that authoritarian attitudes, as measured by Theodore Adorno's famous F-Scale, decrease as a result of military indoctrination. [40] The authors often confess themselves reluctant to reach these conclusions, wonder about the adequacy of the F-scale, and finally speculate that "the concept of the authoritarian military leader may be anchored in an incomplete and somewhat distorted

* *The Professional Soldier,* p. 234; see also Richard Carl Brown, "Social Attitudes of American Generals," unpublished Ph.D. thesis, University of Wisconsin, 1951, p. 38: "[The] basic social attitudes of our military leaders [do] not differ from those possessed by other leaders in American life. Their origins have been essentially the same and the training of the military leader does little to change the social attitudes he already had."

stereotype." [41] In short, the experiments run counter to the assumptions of the experimenters. No one who has ever served in uniform doubts that the army includes men of sadistic inclinations, men who use their authority to abuse their underlings, but the evidence suggests that the discipline of military organization may actually diminish authoritarian tendencies.

The military establishment has, in addition, become increasingly representative of the nation as a whole. C. Wright Mills proved indignantly that the military elite, like business and political elites, is overwhelmingly white, Anglo-Saxon, upper-class and middle-class Protestant. Mills did not note that the democratization of American society is reflected in the transformation of the military elite. The religious denominations now appear among the military elite in very nearly the ratio of the nation at large. Of the generals studied by Brown (from 1898 to 1940), 91 per cent were Protestant and 9 per cent were Catholic. In the West Point class of 1961, 64 per cent were Protestant, 29 per cent were Catholic, 2 per cent were Jewish, and 5 per cent gave "other" or "none" as religious preference. Studies indicate that the upper-class and upper-middle-class domination of West Point, Annapolis, and the Air Force Academy has been broken. And, insofar as can be inferred from names, the West Point Class of 1963 contained 41 cadets whose ancestors came from Southern or Eastern Europe, four whose ancestors are Oriental. (About 9 per cent of the total; German Jewish names not included.) Janowitz concludes that "there is considerable justification for the belief that the military establishment is becoming an avenue for social mobility for those of lower social origin and from new immigrant families." [42]

Although Negroes are under-represented at the service academies, the tendency has been in the right direction. Only three Negroes finished West Point between 1865 and 1898—and none of these rose above lieutenant. Several Negroes are now generals. On the whole, the army's attitude toward Negroes has been in advance of civilian opinion. In World War I, the army accepted segregation and secretly urged the French not to treat Negro troops as equals. The consensus was that the Negro made a poor soldier. In World War II, some Negroes were integrated as platoons in white companies—despite the fact that 74 per cent of Northern-born college-educated white soldiers preferred segregation. Although Negroes did not perform as well as whites, Negroes in integrated units did better than Negroes in segregated ones. When completely integrated forces fought in Korea, Mark Clark wrote that he was wrong in his previous skepticism. And he quoted his former errors at length and praised the new military policy that would help the Negro win "a place he never before held among his fellow Americans." [43] The fact that Negroes are a larger proportion of the professional army than of the population as a whole does not mean that draft boards discriminate against Negroes. Actually, whites are statistically more likely to be conscripted, but many Negroes have chosen to remain in the army because they recognize opportunities not yet available in civilian life.

And Then We Heard the Thunder, John Oliver Killens's militant novel of World War II, dramatizes better than any other work of fiction the humiliations of the American Negro. The anguish of Negro soldiers in the novel comes not from the injustices of the army (which were many) but from the fact that the Negroes expected the military, engaged in a war against Fascism, to act more democratically than the institutions of civilian life. On the question of race relations, at least, the expectation has at last been realized.[44]

The evidence—only a tiny fraction of which can be cited in a single chapter—is conclusive. "While military beliefs about politics remain heavily weighted on the conservative side," writes Janowitz, "the content of conservatism itself has been transformed." [45] The profession "has never been fixated on a feudal myth"; its position on social issues is flexible. "In fact, to date, military conservatism reveals a critical attitude toward contemporary institutions such as would be expected from any effective professional group." [46] What this means is that the military establishment accepts a status quo in the process of slow transformation from Liberal to social democracy. The very fact that the soldier, like the civilian, automatically uses "liberal" and "conservative" in reference to social change rather than to political theory indicates that they are a part of the mainstream and not a countercurrent.

One step further. MacArthur, like the dispossessed generals on the Radical Right, correctly saw the New Deal and subsequent reforms of American society as socialistic. He rather polemically defined socialism as "a centrally controlled economic life [forced] upon all persons in the nation under an authoritarian monoply that is politically managed." [47] What the crusty dispossessed have failed to see is the essential truth of the partisan quip that reminded Eisenhower in election time that he had lived his entire adult life within the paternalistic institutions of the Federal government. The generals stand stiffly as they point in indignation to the wilted moral fiber of those who live at the government's expense. Their allies on the Right, admirers of the military life, declaim against socialism's "regimentation" of our economy.

Have they not missed the point? Is it not obvious that the *implicit* theory of the military establishment today is a pragmatic form of socialism, equidistant from Marxism and from Liberalism? That, by its structure and function, the military assumes a form of social democracy perfectly compatible with the post–New Deal changes in American society? To conventional wisdom, the suggestion is absurd. But the social democratic ideal that defines individual liberty as possible only within an institutional context is far closer to the military ethic than is the Liberal ideal of Emersonian individualism. Ideals of social service and of social responsibility are closer to the military ethic than is the cult of Economic Man, the Market Place, and the Profit Motive. Social democracy's commitment to planning is certainly closer to the military ethic than is the ideology of laissez-faire. The ideology that sees and attempts institutionally to mediate social and economic conflicts is closer to the military ethic than is the ideology that begins with the assumption of universal harmony and ends with the insistence that half the world has to be obliterated in a blast of thermonuclear retribution.

Because the transformation of American society in this century has been from an imperfect Liberal democracy to an imperfect social democracy, the American soldier can for the first time in our history square the dictates of his professional ethic with the accepted values and institutions of our society. Because the soldier has never been at home with the Liberal conception of freedom, he can now contribute immensely to the modern quest for individual liberty within a stable framework of institutional structures. Because the soldier has never had any illusions about the efficacy of unenforced international "law," he can now, if he will, help to develop the international institutions that are the only realistic alternative to the fluctuations of the arms race and the dangerous uncertainties of the Cold War. The opportunities for civil-military co-operation are too important to be lost in a squabble over the "militarism" of the American army.

V

The Revival of Conservative Ideas

1 *Conservatism* Manqué: *Henry Adams*

The Civil War was not caused by economic determinants, except to the degree that slavery was an economic as well as a moral factor in the sectional conflict, but the Civil War did mark the transition of the United States from an overwhelmingly agrarian to a predominantly industrial nation. Barrington Moore, surveying the war in a comparative context that includes analyses of modernization in England, France, China, Japan, and India, comes to the conclusion Charles Beard reached a generation ago: the struggle of 1861–65 was a "Second American Revolution" because the whirlwind unleashed at Sumter swept away the last impediments to industrial capitalism.[1]

Among the most tragic ironies of the time was the ardor with which the Northern and Southern elites went forward to their doom. Francis Parkman, in a series of letters to the *Boston Advertiser,* acclaimed the South because it was "a community essentially military," exempt from the "organized scramble of mean men for petty spoils."[2] He praised the youth of his own "Brahmin caste" because they too showed virility and leadership. The younger Charles Francis Adams, like the younger Oliver Wendell

Holmes, Charles Russell Lowell, and Theodore Winthrop, went off to war. In London, the elder Charles Francis Adams served the Republic which his grandfather, John Adams, had helped to found. Meanwhile, a new generation of rulers laid the framework for their rule. Judge Thomas Mellon of Pittsburgh advised his son to hire a substitute:

> You can learn nothing in the army. . . . In time you will come to understand and believe that a man may be a patriot without risking his own life or sacrificing his health. There are plenty of other lives less valuable or others ready to serve for the love of serving.[3]

James Mellon hired his substitute. John D. Rockefeller, J. Pierpont Morgan, Philip D. Armour, and Jay Gould hired theirs. Mellon made his fortune, and they made theirs. All of them, as well as others such as Jay Cooke and Cornelius Vanderbilt, profited immensely, often at the expense of Northern soldiers whom they sold defective weapons or transported in decrepit ships. While they grew wealthy, Robert Gould Shaw was killed at Fort Wagner and flung in a ditch with the bodies of his Negro troops.*

In retrospect, historians acknowledge Andrew Carnegie's intellectual interests and philanthropic achievements. Although some of the "Robber Barons" dreamed only of loot and gloried at the chance to pillage a corporation into bankruptcy, others proved themselves imaginative, bold, public-spirited, and probably indispensable to the industrial development of the nation. But Henry Adams, upon his return from London (where he had served as his father's private secretary), was not disposed to be charitable toward the new class that had robbed him of his birthright. With the help of his brother, Charles Francis, he turned to journalism and exposed the machinations of Fisk and Gould.

---

* Shaw had recently married Josephine Lowell, James Russell Lowell's niece. At the time of the dedication of St. Gaudens's monument to Shaw, on Boston Common, William James delivered a eulogy. The eulogy, the monument, and Shaw himself now figure in Robert Lowell's poem, "For the Union Dead."

Through most of 1868, Jim Fisk, Jay Gould, Daniel Drew, and Cornelius Vanderbilt had, in various combinations, fought each other for control of the Erie Railway Company. They bribed judges, bought legislators, manipulated stocks and bonds, defrauded each other, and were, apparently, admired by their fellow citizens. "What do I care about the law?" asked Commodore Vanderbilt. "Hain't I got the power?" [4] Charles Francis Adams, in the first of the essays he and Henry collected in *Chapters of Erie* (1871), laments the day:

> Legislative bribery and corruption were, within recent memory, looked upon as antiquated misdemeanors . . . and their revival in the face of modern public opinion was thought to be impossible. In this regard at least a sad delusion was certainly entertained. Governments and ministries no longer buy the raw material of legislation. . . . The same cannot be said of individuals and corporations; for they have of late not infrequently found the supply of legislators in the market even in excess of the demand.[5]

At the conclusion of his 100-page indictment of the Erie's directors, Adams commented, "Ten years ago such revelations as these . . . . would have sent a shudder through the community, and would have placed a stigma on every man who had had to do with them. Now they merely incite others to surpass them by yet bolder outrages and more corrupt combinations." [6] Adams went on, in the volume's third essay, to condemn Fisk and Gould for their attempt to seize the Albany and Susquehanna Railroad. The second essay, "The New York Gold Conspiracy," was Henry's. After his lurid account of the effort, by Fisk, Gould, and President Grant's brother-in-law, to corner the nation's gold supply, he reflected somberly on the fate of "popular institutions."

> For the first time since the creation of these enormous corporate bodies, one of them has shown its power for mischief, and has proved itself able to override and trample on law, custom, decency, and every restraint known to society, without scruple, and as yet without check. The belief is common in America

that the day is at hand when corporations far greater than the Erie—swaying power such as has never in the world's history been trusted in the hands of mere private citizens, controlled by single men like Vanderbilt, or by combinations of men like Fisk, Gould, and Lane, after having created a system of quiet by irresistible corruption—will ultimately succeed in directing government itself.[7]

Adams lived to see the Supreme Court, through its interpretation of the Fourteenth Amendment, endow the corporation with powers undreamed of in the jurisprudence of John Marshall. He lived to see the formation of United States Steel, the first corporation capitalized at over one billion dollars.

He lived also to see the United States demographically transformed by the "new immigration" from Southern and Eastern Europe. Industrialization required labor which millions of Italian Catholics and Russian Jews rushed to undertake. Adams was perhaps less nativistic than most of the "patricians on the defensive" studied by John Higham and Richard Hofstadter in *Strangers in the Land* and *The Age of Reform,* but he was never able to see unionization as a legitimate response to the exploitive power of the capitalists whom he had himself condemned. He was undoubtedly anti-Semitic. "Not a Polish Jew fresh from Warsaw or Cracow," he wrote in *The Education of Henry Adams,* "not a furtive Yacoob or Ysaac still reeking of the Ghetto, snarling a weird Yiddish to the officers of the customs—but had a keener instinct, an intenser energy, and a freer hand than he— American of Americans, with Heaven knew how many Puritans and Patriots behind him. . . ." He refers often in his letters to cupidity of Jews and to their lack of culture, but he was not as restrictionist in immigration policy as his friend Henry Cabot Lodge or as anti-Semitic in his sentiments as his brother Brooks.

By 1879, when Adams published his first novel, the United States had already suffered through the scandals chronicled in *Chapters of Erie,* the depredations of the Tweed Ring, which robbed New York of approximately $200 million, Grant's second term ("The progress of evolution from President Washington to President Grant, was alone evidence enough to upset Darwin" [8]), the contested election of 1876, in which the Democrats accepted a Republican President in return for an end to Reconstruction, and the widespread industrial violence of 1877.

From this congeries of disorders, Adams the novelist chooses one. *Democracy* satirizes the political institutions of the Gilded Age. The heroine is Mrs. Madeleine Lee, widow of a Virginia aristocrat. Bored by life in New York, she ventures to the capital "to see with her own eyes the action of primary forces; to touch with her own hand the massive machinery of society; to measure with her own mind the capacity of the motive power. She was bent upon getting to the heart of the great American mystery of democracy and government." She takes a house in Lafayette Square (where Adams had often visited Charles Sumner), across from the obviously symbolic equestrian statue of Andrew Jackson. She meets Silas P. Ratcliffe, the dominant political figure in Washington, a man known as "the Prairie Giant of Peonia, the Favorite Son of Illinois," a character modeled in part after James Blaine, in part after Roscoe Conkling, with a dash of Stephen A. Douglas. Adams is at his best when he describes Ratcliffe's vanity. At dinner, in a mannered milieu, Mrs. Lee can match wits with the senator, can flatter him with comparisons to Daniel Webster:

> The Senator from Illinois rose to this gaudy fly like a huge, two-hundred-pound salmon; his white waistcoat gave out a mild silver reflection as he slowly came to the surface and gorged the hook. He made not even a plunge, not one perceptible effort to tear out the barbed weapon, but floating gently to her feet, allowed himself to be landed as though it were a pleasure.

The scene is delightful but, in the long run, deceptive. Senator Ratcliffe is neither refined nor subtle of mind, but he is, nonetheless, the most powerful man in the United States. The President, clearly drawn from Ulysses S. Grant, is helpless in his hands.

Ratcliffe is recognized by all insiders as the man in charge.

Mrs. Lee is fascinated by Ratcliffe's energy, by the sense of mastery she feels in his presence. She comes to admire him, until she learns he is no different from the rest. When told how congressmen are bribed, or led, or "driven like Paddy's pig who thought he was going the other way," * she instances Ratcliffe as the exception, only to discover, little by little, that he is completely at home in an environment more corrupt than she had dreamed possible.†

Her sister Sybil, visiting the Lee mansion in Arlington, reads the name of the previous visitor from the guest registry: "Eli M. Grow and lady, Thermopyle Centre." The allusion to the Persian Wars emphasizes the irony. The past has become a spectacle, a grab bag for place names. Sybil wonders, "Did the hosts of Attila write their names on visiting books in the temple of Vesta and the house of Sallust? What a new terror they would have added to the name of the scourge of God! [She] returned to the portico and sat down . . . on the steps." Mrs. Lee is more demoralized still by the degradation of democracy and the grossness of its partisans. She refuses Ratcliffe's hand and determines to find asylum from democracy: " 'I want to go to Egypt,' said Madeleine, still smiling faintly; 'democracy has shaken my nerves to pieces. Oh, what rest it would be to live in the Great Pyramid and look out for ever at the polar star!' "

* The porcine metaphor reappears in *The Education of Henry Adams:* "One day when Adams was pleading with a Cabinet officer for patience and tact in dealing with Representatives, the Secretary impatiently broke out: 'You can't use tact with a Congressman! A Congressman is a hog! You must take a stick and hit him on the snout!' "

† Charles Francis Adams describes his rather similar experiences with "a prominent member of the United States Senate. This Senator is still (1912) alive, though long retired; he has a great reputation for ability, and a certain reputation, somewhat fly-blown, it is true, for rugged honesty. I can only say that I found him an ill-mannered bully, and by all odds the most covertly and dangerously corrupt man I ever had opportunity and occasion carefully to observe in public life. His grudge against the Union Pacific was that it had not retained him—he was not, as a counsel, in its pay." *Autobiography* (Boston, 1916), p. 192.

Although there is much of the author in his portrait of Mrs. Lee, Adams himself was less defeatist than his heroine. He set out to investigate the American past, to discover why it was that the nation his ancestors had founded had no useful place for him. *The Life of Albert Gallatin,* published the same year as *Democracy,* is a brilliant biography of Jefferson's Swiss-born Secretary of the Treasury. Adams valued Gallatin far above Hamilton, in whose works he read "always the same Napoleonic kind of adventuredom." [9] He imagined Gallatin's Geneva as a kind of Boston, and Gallatin as the embodiment of the virtues that characterized John and John Quincy Adams,[10] but Gallatin's career is a morality play that dramatizes the vices of naïve Liberalism. The most poignant passage in the book is a meditation on the transfer of power that took place in 1800, when John Adams gave way to Thomas Jefferson.

> The new political force of which Mr. Jefferson was the guide had no word of sympathy for the vanquished. . . . Even Mr. Gallatin's cooler head felt the power of the strong wine, success. He too believed that human nature was to show itself in new aspects, and that the failures of the past were due to the faults of the past. . . . He had yet to pass through his twelve years of struggle and disappointment in order to learn how his own followers and his own President were to answer his ideal, when the same insolence of foreign dictation and the same violence of a recalcitrant party presented to their and to his own lips the cup of which John Adams was now draining the dregs.[11]

All the rest is an extended commentary on the best laid plans of men.

The nine volumes of Adams's magnificent *History of the United States during the Administrations of Thomas Jefferson and James Madison* (1884–89) orchestrate the same tragic theme. Gallatin, Jefferson, and Madison mean well and fail miserably in their doomed efforts to conduct the affairs of state rationally and pacifically. After six introductory chapters beginning with an intentionally flat statement of the population in 1800 and ending with ruminations about the moral significance of our republican experiment, Adams turned to Thomas Jefferson, to "the man who mounted the steps of the Capitol, March 4, 1801, to claim the place of an equal between Pitt and Bonaparte. . . ." [12] The new Administration determined to avoid domestic discord by a strict interpretation of the Constitution and to "disentangle" the nation from foreign affairs, "except as to commerce, which the merchants will manage the better the more they are left free to manage for themselves. . . ." [13] Adams's chapter on the inauguration ends wryly: "The history of his Administration will show how these principles were applied, and what success attended the experiment." [14] Strict construction led to the Louisiana Purchase, for which there was no constitutional provision. The merchants whom Jefferson hoped to leave "free to manage for themselves" suffered from British and French harassment and then from an embargo which was worse than the ills it was intended to cure. Domestic tranquillity was shattered by a series of impeachments and by Burr's conspiracy. And the war which Jefferson wished at all costs to avoid broke out under his successor.

Architectural imagery is the symbolic stage-set for the ironic drama of political cross-purposes. In 1800,

> The city of Washington, rising in a solitude on the banks of the Potomac, was a symbol of American nationality in the Southern States. The contrast between the immensity of the task and the paucity of the means seemed to challenge suspicion that the nation itself was a magnificent scheme like the federal city, which could show only a few log-cabins and negro quarters where the plan provided for the traffic of London and the elegance of Versailles. . . . The half-finished White House stood in a naked field overlooking the Potomac, with two awkward Department buildings near it, a single row of brick houses and a few isolated dwellings within sight, and nothing more; until across a swamp, a mile and a half away, the shape-

less, unfinished Capitol was seen, two wings without a body, ambitious enough in design to make more grotesque the nature of its surroundings. The conception proved that the United States understood the vastness of their task. . . .[15]

Unfortunately, Congress "doled out funds . . . with so sparing a hand, that their Capitol threatened to crumble in pieces and crush Senate and House under the ruins, long before the building was complete." [16] If anyone could fulfill the Founders' dream of rivaling antiquity's grandiose republicanism, surely it was the statesman who had designed the Virginia capitol from the Maison Carrée at Nîmes and built himself a home that is still one of the architectural wonders of the nation. Fourteen years (and seven volumes) later, the Virginia dynasty's humiliation was complete. Soldiers in the service of George III "burned the Capitol, the White House, and the Department buildings because they thought it proper, as they would have burned a negro kraal or a den of pirates." [17] The enlightened vision of a reasonable polity lay in ashes.

Adams deemed Liberalism to be inadequate, but he did not in his despair become a Conservative. The reasons are in the autobiography. The chief difficulty was that Henry Adams, of all Americans the most likely to develop a sense of the past, looked backward and saw only discontinuity.

The Education of Henry Adams (1907) begins in his grandfather's day, in the Boston that Charles Bulfinch built.

> Under the shadow of Boston State House, turning its back on the house of John Hancock, the little passage called Hancock Avenue runs, or ran, from Beacon Street, skirting the State House grounds, to Mount Vernon Street, on the summit of Beacon Hill.

After contrasting his heritage to that of a hypothetical "Israel Cohen," born in "Jerusalem under the shadow of the Temple and circumcised in the Synagogue," Adams returns again to his "nest of associations," to "the First Church, the Boston State

House, Beacon Hill," and, in the summers, his grandfather's house in Quincy, an old house still furnished with Queen Anne mahogany panels and Louis Seize chairs and sofas. In the nine-volume *History,* Robert Fulton's little steamboat symbolizes the technological forces which Thomas Jefferson could not control; the same forces are, in *The Education,* equally decisive:

> [Henry Adams] and his eighteenth-century, troglodytic Boston were suddenly cut apart—separated forever—in act if not in sentiment, by the opening of the Boston and Albany Railroad; the appearance of the first Cunard steamers in the bay; and the telegraphic messages which carried from Baltimore to Washington the news that Henry Clay and James K. Polk were nominated for the Presidency. This was in May, 1844; he was six years old; his new world was ready for use, and only fragments of the old met his eyes.

Shaken by the machine from his eighteenth-century equilibrium, Adams sought new bearings, sought to run a new order through the old chaos.

In the stateliness of Mount Vernon, Adams found new paradoxes. "People made pilgrimages to Mount Vernon and made even an effort to build Washington a monument." But Virginia roads were bad, and "bad roads meant bad morals." Slavery was wicked and slavery was the cause of the "road's badness which amount to social crime—and yet, at the end of the road and product of the crime stood Mount Vernon and George Washington." The box-hedges and symmetrical buildings remained, but what did they mean? "He never thought to ask himself or his father how to deal with the moral problem that deduced George Washington from the sum of all wickedness."

Equally meaningless were the elaborate neo-classical temples of Chicago's Columbian Exhibition. Seeking answers, and rejecting implicitly the frontier thesis which Frederick Jackson Turner then set forth to the *American Historical Association,* Adams found only questions. If it had been difficult to deduce George Washington "from the sum of all wickedness," how much more difficult to deduce industrial America from the peristylic frenzy of Chicago's grandiose "Court of Honor"! If Bulfinch's State House was "troglodytic" to a child doomed "to play the game of the twentieth" century, then clearly the classic revival of McKim, Mead, and White was a Paleozoic vestige in a nation transformed by steam and electricity.

> One sat down to ponder on the steps beneath Richard Hunt's dome almost as deeply as on the steps of Ara Coeli [where Gibbon had decided to write his decline and fall], and much to the same purpose. Here was a breach of continuity—a rupture in historical sequence!

At length, Henry Adams found himself figuratively "lying in the Gallery of Machines at the Great Exposition of 1900, his historical neck broken by the sudden irruption of forces totally new." The dynamo became the "spool on which to wind the thread of history. . . ." The dynamo and the virgin represented "two kingdoms of force," but Henry Adams could pledge his allegiance to neither. He detailed the architectural wonders of Mont-St.-Michel and Chartres and the architectonics of St. Thomas Aquinas, but he could not follow to the faith that had raised the structures he marveled at.[18] Orestes Brownson, and Adams's own friend, John La Farge, knelt inside, but Adams remained aloof. He established his residence in the splendid double house that H. H. Richardson built for him and John Hay, and he watched Hay and Roosevelt and Root play at power politics, but the lesson of his education is estrangement and alienation. The sense of the past had evaporated. Nothing remained but a residue—the comfortless calculations of the dynamic theory of history.[19]

Returning to New York in 1904, Adams found the skyline "unlike anything man had ever seen—and like nothing he had ever much cared to see." Like Henry James, who returned to the American scene in the same year, he was bewildered by the prospect before him:

The outline of the city became frantic in its effort to explain something that defied meaning. Power seemed to have outgrown its servitude and to have asserted its freedom. The cylinder had exploded, and thrown great masses of stone and steam against the sky.

In the no-man's-land between the two kingdoms of force, between Chartres and the Gallery of Machines, "sensitive and timid natures" wandered in exile, homeless.

Henry Adams termed himself, with an irony that not every reader has caught, a "Conservative Christian Anarchist." Like the Holy Roman Empire of the quip, he deserved none of the terms of the tripartite title. Another of his whimsical appelations, "Unitarian mystic," came closer, and he often called himself a radical, but in truth he was a pessimistic Liberal who understood the ideologies of the century too well to accept any one of them.[20]

Writing from London in 1863, he had described Alexis de Tocqueville and John Stuart Mill as "the two high priests of our faith."

> I have learned to think De Tocqueville my model, and I study his life and works as the Gospel of my private religion. The great principle of democracy is still capable of rewarding a a conscientious servant.[21]

He added then, "And I doubt me much whether the advance of years will increase my toleration of its faults." The years made him more rather than less captious, but he continued restively to assent to democracy because he could not arrive at an alternative. With considerable reluctance, Russell Kirk admits that Adams was not a Conservative: "The blunt nonconformist piety of John Adams gave way to the doubts of John Quincy Adams, the humanitarianism of Charles Francis Adams, the despair of Henry Adams. Belief in Providence, so enduringly rooted in Burke's Conservatism, was lost in the vicissitudes of New England's Conservative thought."[22] Unwilling to assent to political or religious dogmas, Adams felt forced, like a melancholic Emer-

son, to rely upon himself: "Every man with self-respect enough
to become effective," he wrote in *The Education,* "has to account
to himself somehow, and to invent a formula of his own for his
universe, if the standard formulas failed. There, whether finished
or not, education stopped. The formula, once made, could be
but verified." For Adams, the "stupendous failure of Christianity
tortured history" and the nineteenth-century's evolutionary hypothesis was inadequate:

> The old formulas had failed, and a new one had to be made,
> but, after all, the object was not extravagant or eccentric. One
> sought no absolute truth. One sought only a spool on which
> to wind the thread of history without breaking it.

The irony of Conservatism in the Gilded Age is that the man
most richly qualified by heritage and temperament for commitment to its tenets was, at best, a Conservative *manqué.* He was,
more accurately still, a Liberal stripped of illusions—in the tradition of Thomas Jefferson's friendly antagonist from Quincy, Massachusetts.

2 *The Humanist Movement*

The Education of Henry Adams was privately printed in 1907 in
an edition of one hundred copies distributed to friends. Adams's
refusal to allow commercial publication was an implicit recognition of the unpopularity of his ideas. By 1918, however, when *The
Education* was published by the Massachusetts Historical Society,
Americans were less inclined to laugh at prophets of doom.
World War I had awakened millions from the dream of inevitable
progress.

Although Irving Babbitt published his first book in 1908, Humanism—the form taken by his kind of Conservatism—did not
coalesce into a movement until the "return to normalcy" proved
that Americans had failed to understand the lessons of the war.
Through the 1920's, a kind of Gilded Age *redivivus,* the Humanists maintained that the inadequacy of Liberal democracy proved

the validity of Conservative ideas. Civilization might not survive another war like the one concluded at Versailles.

Insisting on the need for clarity of terms, Babbitt and the other Humanists * distinguished "Humanism" from its opposite, "Humanitarianism." The Humanist heeds the "inner voice" of conscience and lives a life of "vital restraint." The Humanist is constantly mindful of what it is that "sets him apart simply as man from other animals." The Humanitarian, on the other hand, loses his humanity in the impossible desire to become divine; he sinks, in the failure of his Faustianism, to the level of bestiality. "A person who has sympathy for mankind in the lump, faith in its future progress, and desire to serve the great cause of this progress, should be called not a humanist, but a humanitarian." [23] The twin sources of this deluded Humanitarianism were Jean-Jacques Rousseau and Francis Bacon, whom Babbitt saw as the origin of what is wrong with Locke.

Rousseau received the greater share of the blame because Romanticism is a greater evil than positivism. *Rousseau and Romanticism* (1919) is Babbitt's most sustained attack, but Rousseau's influence had perverted the nineteenth-century writers studied in *The Masters of Modern French Criticism* (1912) and could be detected in almost every aspect of American education. Against the sentimentality and egotism of Romanticism, Babbitt arrayed the classics of Greece and Rome, of China and ancient India. To them he added the work of Edmund Burke.[24] In *Democracy and Leadership* (1924) he asserted that the political history of the past two hundred years had been a struggle between Burke and Rousseau, between the statesman of limitation and the prophet of the absolute, between the defender of traditional society and the visionary theorist of the self. In his early essay on "The College and the Democratic Spirit," Babbitt held that Burke was correct

---

* In addition to Babbitt and Paul Elmer More, the important Humanists were Harry Hayden Clark, George Roy Elliott, Norman Foerster, Frank Jewett Mather, Jr., Robert Shafer, and Stuart Sherman. Although Louis Mercier included W. C. Brownell in his *Le Mouvement Humaniste aux Etats-Unis* (1928), Brownell was never a member of the group.

to temper liberty by "true restraint." [25] The same Conservative definition of liberty appears in *The New Laokoon* (1910)—liberty is obedience to "a higher law." [26] His most extended discussion, in *Democracy and Leadership*, comes to the same stringent conclusion: "True liberty is not liberty to do as one likes, but liberty to adjust oneself, in some sense of the word, to law. . . . Equality . . . is incompatible with true liberty; for liberty involves an inner working with reference to standards, the right subordination, in other words, of man's ordinary will to a higher will." [27]

On one important issue, however, Babbitt deviated from Conservatism. He could not bring himself to accept Christianity. His lack of faith became, in 1928, the subject of an essay by T. S. Eliot, who had been Babbitt's student at Harvard, whose support in the crusade against modernism Babbitt had counted on. "The problem of humanism," he stated, "is undoubtedly related to the problem of religion." Then, in the rhetorical manner that marks his essays, Eliot asked some questions:

> Is [Humanism], in the end, a view of life that will work by itself or is it a derivative of religion which will work only for a short time in history, and only for a few highly cultivated persons like Mr. Babbitt—whose ancestral traditions, furthermore, are Christian, and who is, like many people, at the distance of a generation or so from definite Christian belief? Is it, in other words, durable beyond one or two generations? *

The answer, which surely surprised no one, was negative. Humanism without religion was an absurdity.

Eliot did not relent. He encouraged Allen Tate to write on the

---

* "The Humanism of Irving Babbitt," *Selected Essays,* 2nd ed. (New York, 1950), p. 420. The essay was originally collected in *For Lancelot Andrewes.* Eliot continued the attack in "Second Thoughts about Humanism," *Selected Essays,* pp. 429–38, but moderated his voice in "Religion without Humanism," in *Humanism and America,* pp. 105–12. After More's death, Eliot wrote in the *Princeton Alumni Weekly* (February 5, 1937) that More and Babbitt were "the two *wisest* men that I have known." Quoted in Arthur Hazard Dakin, *Paul Elmer More,* (Princeton, 1960), p. 386.

Humanists and published Tate's extremely hostile essay in *Criterion* (Eliot's own journal, published in London). Tate was more specific in his analysis and more caustic, but he came to the same conclusion: "The assumptions of this essay are that Humanism is not enough, and that if the values for which the Humanist pleads are to be made rational, even intelligible, the prior condition of an objective religion is necessary. . . . Religion is the sole technique for the validating of values." [28] The inquiry into the viability of Humanism without religion ended with Babbitt isolated, and hurt. His retort to his critics was that the test of a religion is the behavior of its adherents, and that Buddhism "has had as many saints as Christianity and . . . has, moreover, been less marred than Christianity by intolerance and fanaticism." [29] Paul Elmer More recalled, after Babbitt's death, an incident that suggests that his friend's proposed alliance between Humanism and religion was a bit of *Realpolitik;* Babbitt would stop on the street in Cambridge, point to a nearby church, and exclaim, "There is the enemy! there is the thing I hate!" [30] The oddity is that the teacher of French literature who loathed French literature should also be the Conservative who says of Christianity, "Ecrasez l'infame!"

More himself, although he began his career as a latter-day Thoreau and served for a time as an editor of *The Nation,* became a lesser but more consistent Conservative. The early volumes of the Shelburne Essays, named for the small town in New Hampshire to which More retired "as a hermit after a mild Epicurean fashion of my own," [31] are broadly humanistic in the ordinary sense of the word. They reveal an openness to a remarkable range of human experience. With time, however, the tone changes, the line hardens; there was a great deal which became alien to More. By the Sixth Series (1909), Rousseau and other humanitarians are thoroughly objectionable.

That the milieu and the moment had something to do with More's qualms is likely. Reviewing two books on socialism, he admitted that "the thought of this discontent, gnawing at the very heart of our civilization, strikes me with a kind of vague terror, as if I had strayed into a land swept by armies clashing ignorantly in the night, or had fallen into some dream of the streets of Troy where friend and foe surged together under the same standards." [32] The Eighth Series, published in 1913, is entitled *The Drift of Romanticism*. More recognizes the importance of Babbitt's "inner check," but he is unready to rely upon it. Tradition, after all, is "the experience of a society . . . stored up for use by what may be called the objective memory," [33] but most men are untouched by tradition. There's the difficulty; the remedy is not unexpected—society must, for its own preservation, create "external checks in the form of government." [34] Men are, once again, to be restrained to their true liberty.

The next volume, *Aristocracy and Justice,* is openly and dogmatically political. Burke's *Reflections* is lauded as a fountain of political wisdom. His notion of aristocracy, a class trained from birth to rule, a class "of those whose views [are] broadened by the inherited possession of privilege and honours," seems attractive. [35] The tone itself becomes an echo of Burke's:

> The enormous preponderance of studies that deal with the immediate questions of economics and government inevitably results in isolating the student from the great inheritance of the past; the frequent habit of dragging him through the slums of sociology, instead of making him at home in the society of the noble dead, debauches his mind with a flabby, or inflames it with a fanatic, humanitarianism. [36]

The problem of unionization in the mines of Colorado is simply dealt with: "To the civilized man *the rights of property are more important than the right to life."* [37] (The emphasis here is More's.) More does not go into the various forms in which property is held, or ask if the modern corporation is what Locke had in mind when he wrote of man's mixing his labor with the products of the earth.

Justice is sternly defined as the "inner state of the soul when, under the command of the will to righteousness, reason guides and the desires obey." [38] The just man has a social obligation to coerce the unjust man.

The last volume of Shelburne Essays, *A New England Group and Others,* is a world away, in its tone, from the first. Jonathan Edwards, despite his obsession with evil, is deemed a great theologian, but Emerson, the central figure in our literature, is faulted for his blindness to evil: "Hence it is that he often loses value for his admirers in proportion to their maturity and experience." [39] More's own maturity and experience leads him firmly to renounce the skepticism of Henry Adams, whose ancestors had discarded "tradition and authority and form and symbol" in order to affirm the transcendental values of their religious faith.

> But the liberty of denying may itself become a habit. The intellectual history of New England is in fact the record of the encroachment of this liberty on the very affirmation for which it was at first the bulwark. By a gradual elimination of its positive content the faith of the people had passed from Calvinism to Unitarianism, and from this to free thinking, until in the days of our Adams there was little left to the intellect but a great denial. [40]

More himself preferred a great affirmation. His interest in social issues gave way quickly to his final concern, the evolution of Greek thought from the Dialogues of Plato to the triumph of Christianity at the Council of Chalcedon, which Plato's philosophy had faintly adumbrated. A volume of essays, *The Sceptical Approach to Religion* (1934), is an academic version of the confident placards posted at religious centers on college campuses: "Is Christianity Outmoded?" (The answer is usually negative.) Approaching religion skeptically, More does Descartes one better and shows that doubt leads inevitably to the Incarnation, which is the central truth of all human experience. The last years of More's life were given over to the four massive volumes of *The Greek Tradition* (and to a pair of complementary volumes which appeared in 1931). The reader who struggles the length of the six volumes learns what he learns from T. S. Eliot's *Four Quartets:* "Not Christianity alone is at stake in our acceptance or rejection of the Incarnation, but religion itself." [41] More, however, turns the tables on Eliot, whose own orthodoxy is questioned. More charged, in a letter, that Eliot's God was "an abortion sprung of the unholy coupling of the Aristotelian Absolute and the Phoenician Moloch. . . ." [42] More's orthodoxy, on the other hand, has satisfied Russell Kirk, who has called him our most eminent Anglican thinker. [43]

At the end of his life, More wondered if he had not been mistaken to have remained in America. He wrote to Philip Richards in 1935, "More and more, year by year, the regret grows on me that, when I gave up my office work in New York, I did not transplant myself to England." [44] He lived in Princeton, but there is a sense in which he lapsed into New England ways, not the ways of Emerson's day but of the late seventeenth century. His works are Jeremiads, a call to repentance. Like most prophets, he was unheard. It seems safe to assert that he is, today, unread.*

* The fate of Ralph Adams Cram has been starker still. Scarcely mentioned in Kirk's *Conservative Mind,* he was beyond doubt the most Conservative of our major architects, the one most touched by a sense of the past. For him, ecclesiastical architecture *had* to be Gothic because it was part of what he called the "sacramental view of life." [45] Gothic "is the fully developed expression of Christianity." [46] For him, the past was truly prescriptive. The "Great Thousand Years" [47] that stretched from 500 A.D. to 1500 A.D. were a period of "High Democracy" from which the West has declined. The Middle Ages were an age when every man was able to fulfill the potential of his personality in a unified, hierarchical, traditionalist, Christian community. The Renaissance, on the other hand, was a "cockatrice of neo-paganism [hatched] from the egg of Christian civilization." [48] The Reformation was a grisly beast that destroyed masterpieces of Christian art and spawned Calvinism, "the most flagrant heresy Christianity has had to record." [49] The French Revolution was, predictably, a catastrophe. The incomparable horrors of 1914–18 were the ineluctable result of generations of materialism, but the calamity brought also the hope of regeneration. Cram's contributions were literary and architectural. He called for the erection of walled towns where mankind might live as well as it had in the Middle Ages, with obligatory guild membership, with a civic hierarchy composed of apprentices, journeymen, masters, and knights, with a single church, and without the intermarriage of "peoples of every known blood, race and status [which] can only appear the blackest and most imbecile crime in the human calendar." [50] He

3 *Our European Visitor*

Of the great American philosophers, George Santayana was the most Conservative and the least American. Born in Madrid in 1863, he was named Jorge Agustín Nicolás Santayana y Borrás. He was transplanted, in 1872, to Boston, where his mother had gone three years earlier to be with relatives of her first husband, George Sturgis. Santayana was and felt himself to be the child of two cultures. He was a Latin thinker intellectually akin to Plato and Lucretius. He was, at the same time, a Puritan *malgré lui*. The psychic division is projected and dramatized in his novel, *The Last Puritan* (1936), in the characters of Oliver Alden and Mario Van de Weyer.

He was critical of his American hosts and chastized them for the vapidities of the genteel tradition, but his complaints were seldom unsympathetic ones. His essay on Emerson is written in sorrow, with none of the easy contempt expressed by lesser Conservatives.[52] His various attacks on Whitman, whom he characterized as one of the poets of barbarism, were never without an acknowledgment of what it was that Whitman, better than any other poet, had done:

> Never, perhaps, has the charm of uniformity in multiplicity been felt so completely and so exclusively. Everywhere it greets us with a passionate preference; not flowers but leaves of grass, not music but drum-taps, not composition but aggregation, not the hero but the average man, not the crisis but the vulgarest moment; and by this resolute marshalling of nullities, by this effort to show us everything as a momentary pulsation of a liquid and structureless whole, he profoundly stirs the imagination.[53]

built a series of buildings to house society's Conservative institutions—West Point's Post Headquarters, Princeton's Graduate College, and the still unfinished Cathedral of St. John the Divine in New York.[51] Cram himself can hardly be blamed if the army has ceased to be a stronghold of Conservatism, if American universities have become centers of dissent, if the churches of the United States (or some of them) have turned again to the Social Gospel.

Santayana earned the right to criticize character and opinion in the United States.

It was not, of course, just the United States. Even in England, the traditional asylum of American Conservatives, he found that Liberalism had created "a Babel of false principles and blind cravings, a zoological garden of the mind." [54] The age was wrong. "The Liberal age in which I was born and the Liberal circles in which I was educated flowed contentedly towards intellectual dissolution and anarchy." [55] He loved his friend and colleague William James and paid him many tributes, and yet he wondered at his ingenuousness at the time of the American seizure of the Philippines. James "cried disconsolately that he had lost his country, when his country, just beginning to play its part in the history of the world, appeared to ignore an ideal that he had innocently expected would always guide it, because this ideal had been eloquently expressed in the Declaration of Independence." [56] James had, of course, judged as a rationalist, without comprehending the place of nations in their historical context. At his best, the Liberal imagines that nations have already institutionalized his utopian dreams; at his worst, the Liberal imposes on all civilization "a single cheap and dreary pattern." [57]

Liberalism erred also in its conception of liberty. Santayana's criticism here resembles Eliot's indictment of secular humanism. Liberalism was parasitic upon the customs and codes of the past. It depended upon the Conservative civilization that it stigmatized. "If Liberalism had been a primitive system, with no positive institutions behind it, it would have left human genius in the most depressed and forlorn condition." [58] Liberalism has been fortunate in its inheritance of viable institutions, but it is weakened internally by an illusory theory of liberty that fails to consider the myriad ways civilized men are restricted, conditioned, and shaped by their social environment, by their bodies and brains. Liberalism prided itself in trivial differentiations, in eccentricities, in meaningless choices, but "it is in the subsoil of uniformity, of tradition, of dire necessity that human welfare is rooted, together with wisdom and unaffected art, and the flowers of culture that do not draw their sap from that soil are only paper flowers." [59] Liberty follows from the recognition of necessity. But this insight did not lead Santayana to asceticism. He did not define liberty as its opposite. The liberty which follows from the recognition of necessity is the end that must be pursued. "The substance and joy of liberty begin only when the well-integrated powers of the psyche find or establish a world in which they bear their specific and appropriate fruit." [60] When Santayana writes of the ideals of the Greek philosophers, he emphasizes the glory of the liberation rather than the restraint which makes the liberation possible:

> Mankind has continued to run wild and like barbarians to place freedom in their very wildness, till we can hardly conceive the classic assumption of Greek philosophers and cities, that true liberty is bound up with an institution, a corporate scientific discipline, necessary to set free the perfect man, or the god, within us.[61]

Santayana did not for a moment believe that all men are by nature equal in their abilities, but he never assumed that the inequalities of our social existence are an exact copy of natural inequality. He knew that life is hard and that convention can make it harder still. The "sly injustice of men" is more difficult to bear than the "brutal but innocent injustice of nature" because the enforced privation of some enables others to "be exempt from care and to live like the gods in irresponsible ease." [62]

For the pretensions of hereditary aristocracy, Santayana had strong words. "It is no loss of liberty," he wrote, "to subordinate ourselves to a natural leader," [63] but the natural aristocracy of one generation "declines into a conventional and baseless authority." [64] Achieved status turns quickly into the dysfunctional privilege of ascription: "As a rule, men's station determines their occupation without their gifts determining their station. Thus stifled ability in the lower orders, and apathy or pampered incapacity in the higher, unite to deprive society of its natural leaders." [65] The best government would be a timocracy—the rule of merit. "People would be born equal, but they would grow unequal, and the only equality subsisting would be equality of opportunity." [66] This is the ideal type of government, but it cannot be realized. The best we can hope for is a society of many institutions, most of which recruit leaders from their own ranks, in the manner of armies, universities, and churches. Timocratic institutions might then act as a check upon parliamentary government. It is a pessimistic view, and even a Conservative one, but perhaps not as antidemocratic as has been charged.*

Santayana was not ready to trust blindly in prescription, in the determinations of history, nor did he place his faith in Revelation. It was not the life of faith that he wished to conserve; it was the life of reason. "The life of reason is a heritage and exists only through tradition," [67] but the tradition which preserves human rationality and the record of achievement is similar to rather than identical with the tradition of Burke.

Russell Kirk's claim that Burke "strides through Santayana's books" is supported by reference to the title, *Winds of Doctrine,* but the phrase is one Burke and Santayana both quote from a third influential writer, St. Paul.[68] The Greek world is the point of departure for Santayana, but it is not the world of the New Testament and the Church Fathers. It is the *polis* in which Plato, Aristotle, and Epictetus are notable personages.

Santayana was moved by the achievements of Greece and Rome because the philosophical basis of his Conservatism was naturalistic rather than religious in the traditional sense. He was a materialist who brought Plato's Forms down into the world of nature. He denied them transcendent existence, and he denied the theological claims of Christianity. When T. S. Eliot praised Dante's Catholicism at the expense of Shakespeare's stoicism, Santayana murmured that Dante's philosophy had a major flaw—it wasn't true.[69]

---

* *Dominations and Powers* (1951), Santayana's last, difficult book on political theory, came out after David Spitz's discussion in *Patterns of Anti-Democratic Thought.*

Santayana valued traditional faiths for the poetry in them. To say this is not to trivialize the philosophy, for poetry was central to it. Santayana's view was Matthew Arnold plus a little whimsy. His first five books are poetry or interpretations of poetry, a sign of earnestness and concern. Religion and poetry are identical in origin and in mode, but "religion is the poetry in which we believe." [70] In this sense, all religions were poems to him. Summarizing the central thesis of *Interpretations of Poetry and Belief,* Richard C. Lyon comments,

> The dignity and worth of religions are made manifest when we understand them as symbolic interpretations of the meanings and values of human life; but when a religion grows assertive and insists upon the Fact, its conflict with science or with other sects may lead it to militancy, and in asserting its exclusive rightness it too easily passes to a social or political tyranny.[71]

Santayana was certain that "beauty is a pledge of the possible conformity between the soul and nature, and consequently a ground of faith in the supremacy of the good," [72] but he did not confuse poetic with scientific truth and scorned the fanatics who did.

He was always too much of a materialist to be patient with mysticism. T. S. Eliot wrote in "Burnt Norton," the first of the *Four Quartets,* of the mystic moment in the rose garden when time was intersected by eternity:

> Sudden in a shaft of sunlight
> Even while the dust moves
> There rises the hidden laughter
> Of children in the foliage
> Quick now, here, now, always—
> Ridiculous the waste sad time
> Stretching before and after.

Unsanctified time was for Santayana sad, perhaps, but neither ridiculous nor a waste. Although Santayana admired the *Four*

Quartets,[73] the experience of the mystic was for him an unjustified repudiation of our physical natures. "Since spirit is an emanation of natural life there would be impiety on its part in flouting or denying its own source . . ." [74] Protesting both the mystic's flight from the here and the now and the extreme sceptic's doubt of the very existence of the universe, he defended always, with sly eloquence, the material world which common sense and animal faith had taken, perhaps a little too unreflectively, for granted.

Many a modern in the century since Renan has denied the divinity of Christ and praised the ethics of Jesus. Not Santayana. Here too, he is on the side of the Greeks. He was ready, in his Hellenism, to honor sexuality and to condemn even the sacrosanct concept of chastity. He commented with irony that it was not reasonable "to dismiss all ideals but the Christian and then invoke Christian patience to help us endure the consequent evils, which are thus declared to be normal." [75]

> The world may have little in it that is good: granted. But that little is really and inalienably good. Its value cannot be destroyed because of the surrounding evil. But the greatest of all evils is surely that lunacy that convinces us that this little good is not good, and subverts natural standards in favor of unnatural and irrational standards. It is a form of insanity.[76]

He was given to jests—"There is no God and Mary is His Mother"—but his great book, *The Life of Reason,* is Stoic rather than Christian. He was a man of "natural piety and courage.[77] He was Conservative enough to accept institutionalized Catholicism, *cum grano salis.*

Born in the land of Seneca, he returned to live in that of his favorite philosophical poet, Lucretius. Like Henry James and T. S. Eliot, he abandoned America to its democratic devices. He domiciled himself in Italy and died, in 1952, among the believing, uncomprehending Sisters of Santo Stefano. Wallace Stevens's poem, "To An Old Philosopher in Rome," and Robert Lowell's, "For George Santayana," are two indications that we Americans have not forgotten our guest.

4 *Knowledge Carried to the Heart: The Agrarians.**

In 1930, the year that Norman Foerster edited a controversial collection of essays by Irving Babbitt, Paul Elmer More, and other Humanists,[78] twelve Southerners in a similarly polemical mood published *I'll Take My Stand*. The young men † who belligerently quoted "Dixie" in the title of their collective manifesto were Conservative, literary, and important. Their book is a defense of regionalism by men not all of whom had spoken very warmly of their region. Allen Tate had written, only five years earlier, that the "Old South has degenerated into and survives only as a sentiment susceptible of no precise definition." Its people, Tate charged, were gracious rather than intelligent and unable to see "their cultural limitations critically enough to be creatively aware of their imperfections. . . ." [79] There was little of this kind of criticism in 1930.

John Crowe Ransom, Allen Tate, Donald Davidson, and Robert Penn Warren, all of whom had contributed to the Nashville poetry magazine, *The Fugitive* (1922–25), were annoyed by Northern self-righteousness, especially raucous when the Scopes Trial gave H. L. Mencken and others a chance to mock the Fundamentalism of the hill country. The Agrarians were upset by the wide-spread Southern surrender to Northern ideals of industrial progress. The University of North Carolina had long been contaminated by Liberalism; in 1926, their departmental chairman, Edwin Mims, published *The Advancing South*. It was Liberalism too close to home.

They were intemperate in their response and they have been

---

* Portions of this section are taken from "The Agrarians Again," *Kenyon Review,* XXVIII (1966), 548–53.

† They were John Crowe Ransom, Donald Davidson, Frank Lawrence Owsley, John Gould Fletcher, Lyle H. Lanier, Allen Tate, Herman Clarence Nixon, Andrew Nelson Lytle, Robert Penn Warren, John Donald Wade, Henry Blue Kline, and Stark Young.

dealt with sternly by literary historians,* but one must remember the year, 1930. Hungry men watched food burn and the wretched unemployed were told by President Hoover, in a burst of mortuary optimism, that jobs aplenty would be available when the present generation of jobholders died. To understand why men might be disillusioned with Wall Street and Washington and the dream of the Industrial Millennium, one need but look at the faces of the sharecroppers in the photographs by Margaret Bourke-White and Walker Evans.

Northern society was condemned by the Agrarians in language that might have been drawn from George Fitzhugh. Industrial capitalism was criticized by them more severely than by the Marxists, who saw in their less polemical moods that bourgeois capitalism and Liberal democracy were necessary stages on the road to socialism. The Agrarians insisted that capitalism had reduced the masses "to a state of abject economic dependence" and perverted the elite into "industrialists in art" who produced for the market rather than for the greater glory of God.[80] The indictment was comprehensive; the bill was drawn against accessories and accomplices. "We shall not," wrote John Gould Fletcher, "reproach our own mountaineer, poor white folk, for their little schooling and simpler manners, and for lacking those arts and graces that make the public-school product of New York City or Chicago a behaviorist, an experimental scientist in sex and firearms, a militant atheist, a reader of detective fiction, and a good salesman."[81]

Denunciation of modernism was only half the story. The Agrarians had an alternative to disaster. They urged, in econom-

---

* John L. Stewart, whose *The Burden of Time* is the best study of the group, is caustic about their political and social ideas. Theodore Karanikas prefaces *Tillers of a Myth* by asserting that their "hard-headed" Conservatism "could hold its own in debate with Liberalism, rationalism, democracy, or any other offshoot of the idea of progress." He then quarrels with them, often sarcastically, on every major issue. Virginia Rock's "The Making and Meaning of *I'll Take My Stand*," an unpublished Ph.D. dissertation (Minnesota, 1961), ought to be more generally available.

ics, that commercial agriculture be replaced by subsistence farming. There had to be a recovery of the pre-industrial economy. Specifically, their program was set forth in Herman Clarence Nixon's contribution to *I'll Take My Stand,* in Troy Cauley's *Agrarianism: A Program for Farmers* (1935), and in the books of Herbert Agar, with whom Allen Tate edited *Who Owns America?* (This collection of essays, published in 1936, includes chapters by eight of the twelve who contributed to the earlier book—Davidson, Lanier, Lytle, Owsley, Ransom, Wade, Warren, and Tate himself.) The most succinct summary of Agrarian economics is one Owsley published in *The American Review,* a magazine hospitable to Agrarians, to Humanists, and to the English Distributists (e.g. Hilaire Belloc): [82]

> The five pillars on which it would appear that an agrarian society must rest are: (1) The restoration of the people to the land and the land to the people . . . ; (2) The preservation and restoration of the soil . . . ; (3) The establishment of a balanced agriculture where subsistence crops are the first consideration and the money crops are of secondary importance; (4) The establishment of a just political economy, where agriculture is placed upon an equal basis with industry, finance, and commerce; (5) The creation of regional governments possessed of more autonomy than the states. . . . *

The Agrarians understood perfectly well that the subsistence farmer's lot is not easy. When Andrew Lytle urged Southerners to emulate the runt pig and suck hard at the hind tit, he had no illusions about nature's bounty.[83] Life on the land promised little, but at least the promise was kept.

The main argument was, however, moral and aesthetic rather than economic. "Uppermost in our minds," remembered David-

* "The Pillars of Agrarianism," *American Review,* IV (1935), 546–7. The last point was a favorite with Donald Davidson, who followed William Y. Elliott, a Harvard political scientist who had been one of the Fugitives but not an Agrarian. See Davidson's *The Attack on Leviathan: Regionalism and Nationalism in the United States* (Chapel Hill, 1938), chap. 5; and Elliott's *The Need for Constitutional Reform* (New York, 1935).

son in 1935, "was our feeling of intense disgust with the spiritual disorder of modern life—its destruction of human integrity and its lack of purpose. . . ." [84] Although the name of Jefferson moves in and out of the essays on economics, it is clear that the return to the soil was also a return to the values of a traditional community pervaded by a sense of the past. [85]

Tate wrote to Davidson in 1928 that "this quest of the past is something we all share, but it is most acute in me—more so than in you, I suspect." [86] The letter, written in accompaniment of Tate's most famous poem, "Ode to the Confederate Dead," can be taken as a commentary on many of Tate's poems, on his novel, and on the biographies of Stonewall Jackson and Jefferson Davis which Tate published in 1928 and 1929.

The first of the *Selected Poems* is "The Mediterranean." The poem derives from a seaside picnic with the novelist whose life linked James and the Agrarians—Ford Madox Ford. The somber tone is set by the epigraph from Virgil: "Quem das finem, rex magne, dolorum?" The speaker thinks of Aeneas, of his own forefathers, and of the westward course of empire.

> What country shall we conquer, what fair land
> Unman our conquest and locate our blood?
> We've cracked the hemispheres with careless hand!
> Now, from the Gates of Hercules, we flood
>
> Westward, westward till the barbarous brine
> Whelms us to the tired land where tasseling corn,
> Fat beans, grapes sweeter than muscadine
> Rot on the vine: in that land were we born.

The hints of doom ("unman," "tired," "rot") are developed in "Aeneas at Washington." In that poem, the Trojan prince remembers that "time when civilization / Run by the few fell to the many." He had bravely set his father on his shoulders and started anew, in Italy and then again—in Tate's imagination—in America. Now he knows the fate of men's hopes. Contemplating the capitol by the Potomac and the decay of another dream, he thinks dourly of men's folly, of fallen Troy, of "what we had built her for."

"The Ode to the Confederate Dead," a speculative and some-times incoherent affirmation of "knowledge carried to the heart," is less impressive than these (and other) poems, less impressive than Tate's single novel, *The Fathers* (1938), which deserves the attention it has only recently received.[87] "The individual quality of a man [is] bound up with his kin and the 'places' where they lived." This is the narrator's conviction, and the novel is one of family and place, especially Pleasant Hill—the symbolic mansion. The impulse to order is beautifully captured in a single image, when the narrator looks at wallpaper with Sappho and Alcaeus in a landscape: "The broken column in the distance I had al-ways wanted to pick up and restore to its place." But the family is scattered, the mansion is burned, and the South is destroyed by Yankee power and the "innate evil of man's nature."

Tate's use of the familiar symbol of the ancestral home is simi-lar to Ransom's in "Old Mansion." In that poem, Ransom's speaker approaches, "as an intruder," a Southern manor in de-cay. Rudely denied entrance, he realizes what might have been and now can never be: "I went with courage shaken / To dip, alas, into some unseemlier world." The poem antedates the Agrarians' collective effort to salvage something from the ruin.

The past was, of course, selectively recaptured. The Old South was reconstructed by the Agrarians as an image of European society. "The South was the last stronghold," wrote Tate in his biography of Jefferson Davis, "of European civilization in the western hemisphere, a Conservative check upon the restless ex-pansiveness of the industrial North."[88] This may undervalue the Conservatism of Latin America and of French Canada, but it does indicate what the Agrarians looked for. Tate repeated him-self and grew more emphatic in *I'll Take My Stand:* "The South could be ignorant of Europe because it *was* Europe. . . ."[89] Ransom, who was equally committed to "a certain terrain, a certain history, and a certain inherited way of living," agreed that the "South is unique on this continent for having founded and defended a culture which was according to the European principles of culture. . . ." [90] There had been engendered in the Old South "that famous, or infamous, European Conservatism, which will appear stupid, necessarily, to men . . . in a state of arrested adolescence." [91]

It is no accident that the single most important influence on the social and literary criticism of the Agrarians was T. S. Eliot. Ransom, who did not at first share Tate's enthusiasm for Eliot, eventually came almost to parody the notorious credo that prefaces *For Lancelot Andrewes*. "I would covet," said Ransom, "a program . . . something like this: In manners, aristocratic; in religion, ritualistic; in art, traditional. . . ." [92]

If one assumes that "manners" means something more than its trivial significance, one suspects that Ransom and Tate looked to a natural aristocracy to lead society. Tate, at least, was explicit. "The institution of slavery was a positive good only in the sense that Calhoun had argued that it was: it had become a necessary element in a stable society. He had argued justly that only in a society of fixed classes can men be free. Only men who are socially as well as economically secure can preserve the historical sense of obligation." [93] There are moments when Tate's two biographies breathe the spirit of Fitzhugh's *Cannibal's All!* The North pursued an erroneous concept of freedom because too much was left to the individual. "For society as a whole the modern system is probably inferior to that of slavery; the classes are not so closely knit; and the employer feels responsible to no law but his own desire. Industrialism comes in the end to absentee landlordism on a grand scale . . ." [94] The Civil War is simplified in an interesting way: "The issue was class rule and religion *versus* democracy and science." [95] Quoting William Harper on society's need for leadership, Tate commented that the sentiments might have come from the works of Irving Babbitt. [96] There are many sentences in Tate's early books of which the same might be said.

Although most of the Agrarians had something to say about the importance of Christianity, Ransom supplied the most extended analysis in his comment on ritualism in religion. *God Without Thunder* (1930) is an Old-Testament denunciation of Liberal Christianity and a fervent appeal for a return to the faith of our fathers—whatever that faith may have been. Ransom, concluding his book, sounds a Conservative version of Eisenhower's undirected piety. The latter had called on his fellow citizens to attend the church of their choice; Ransom asks, "With whatever religious institution a modern man may be connected, let him try to turn it back towards orthodoxy." [97]

What of the third part of Ransom's credo? What of traditionalism in art? Ransom had certainly *begun* his poetic career with traditional forms and traditionally Romantic themes. His first volume, which T. S. Eliot recommended for English publication, includes "An American Addresses Philomela," which relies on one of the legends Eliot worked into the fabric of *The Waste Land:*

> Not to these shores she came! this other Thrace,
> Environ barbarous to the royal Attic.
> How could her delicate dirge run democratic,
> Delivered in a boundless cloudless public place
> To a hypermuscular race?

The tendency of Ransom's poetry, like that of Tate and like the novels of Robert Penn Warren, was certainly in the direction of modernism, but the Agrarians were distinctly Conservative in their literary theories, in their contributions to the body of critique and polemic called "New Criticism" from Ransom's use of the term in the title of his study of I. A. Richards, T. S. Eliot, and Yvor Winters.

Robert Gorham Davis, who finds the New Criticism a derivation from Joseph de Maistre and Charles Maurras, lists "related terms of honor" and "related terms of rejection and contempt." [98]

TERMS OF HONOR	TERMS OF REJECTION AND CONTEMPT
authority	Liberalism
hierarchy	naturalism
Catholicism	scientism
aristocracy	individualism
tradition	equalitarianism
absolutes	progress
dogma	Protestantism
truths	pragmatism
	personality

It was no quirk that made Basil Willey's *The Seventeenth-Century Background* an assigned test for all English majors in the day of the New Criticism's hegemony. Willey is part of an English group of literary Anglicans that included T. S. Eliot, C. S. Lewis, and Dorothy Sayers.[99] In his books, Willey accuses science of the murder of poetry. Francis Bacon and the Royal Society are major culprits, and another of the villains is, of course, John Locke, whose empiricism gave the death-blow to the poetic imagination.

But how precisely are the literary concerns of the New Criticism connected to the political concerns of Conservatism? In what sense is the highly formalistic New Criticism an appropriate expression of the Conservative imagination? The answer is difficult and at least one student of the problem has given up in despair. Theodore Karanikas finds no relationship between the literary and the social criticism. He notes that the New Critics tended, as did Eliot, to lament the loss of tradition, fixed convention, and religious belief, but he finds that "concern over these losses seems quite removed from *textual analysis, or artistic autonomy, or formal aesthetics*—three of the major locutions with which the New Critics are usually identified." [100]

The connection, implicit in the work of the Humanists, is close to the surface in Ransom's essay, "Forms and Citizens," in which he holds that a "natural affiliation binds together the gentleman, the religious man, and the artist—punctilious characters, all of them, in their formalism." [101] After his tripartite credo (aristocracy, ritualism, tradition), Ransom continued, "The word for our generation in these matters is 'formal.' " [102] Ransom's comments can be expanded upon. Conservatism is almost always politically formalistic because institutional structures, without which Conservatism is impossible, are by definition forms of behavior transmissible from generation to generation. Conservatism assumes social forms, and these in turn presume a shared consciousness of symbolic action in two senses of the term, as meaningful behavior (à la Max Weber [103]) and as art. Simply to "go through the forms" is to acknowledge, however reluctantly, one's place in a social system, one's role in the institutional drama. The tendency of democratic movements, on the other hand, is to emphasize in politics and in art the spirit rather than the letter, the content rather than the form. There is a profound insight in T. S. Eliot's witticism, "The spirit killeth, but the letter giveth life." [104] Few formulations show as concisely the difference between the Christianity of St. Paul and that of T. S. Eliot.

The poet of democracy, like the politician, simplifies his form, amplifies his content, and hopes to communicate to all. In Ernst Troeltsch's terms, the poets and the political leaders of democracy are prophets rather than priests. Superficially viewed, the poetry of Walt Whitman and of T. S. Eliot seem similiar. They are experimental poets; they write metrically irregular and generally unrhymed poems. But Eliot's poems are made from other poems that are definitely *not* "on the page" in the sense that a poem by Whitman *is*. Eliot wrote allusively and conventionally in that he played traditional forms off against modern content. Of him, one can declare that "not only the best but the most individual parts of his work may be those in which the dead poets, his ancestors, assert their immortality most vigorously." [105] He aimed to embed in his work the history of the English language; Whitman coined words, counterfeited them, threw them away, and sounded his "barbaric yawp over the roofs of the world." All poems are by definition verbal forms, but Eliot's are formalistic and Whitman's are not. Eliot's demand of the reader a body of knowledge as they implore assent to a set of values.

Textual analysis is a part of the New Criticism because the modern reader (or at least the contemporary student of literature) is liable to be ignorant of traditional forms, conventions, devices, and even information. Artistic autonomy is called for because the moral significance of some works are taken for granted (i.e. they affirm Christian values) and the moral significance of other works is objectionable (e.g. proletarian literature). Artistic autonomy is the literary equivalent of the Conservative's call for an end to "politics" and an acceptance of society as the Conservative wants it. The theory of the New Criticism is anti-didactic, but in practice the New Critics were moralists, and strict ones.

The New Criticism is, then, the continuation of Conservatism. Ironically, it has conquered the classrooms only after becoming standardized, mass-produced, handbooked, and debased. Millions of students have now been trained to appreciate at least some of the poetic complexities once reserved for the educated minority. The New Critics, willingly or unwillingly, have done for our time what Matthew Arnold hoped to do for his. The net effect of their work is incalculable, but it must be, as Arnold hoped poetry's future would be, immense.

VI

The Present and the Future

1 *New Conservatism*

Donald Davidson remains an unreconstructed Rebel and Cleanth Brooks fights a guerrilla war against the New York Literary Establishment, which has not responded to the Conservative streak in William Faulkner,[1] but most of the Agrarians have made their peace with modernism and modified their political views in the direction of social democracy. When Russell Kirk published *The Conservative Mind* in 1953, John Crowe Ransom all but dismissed the book as a waste of time: "Burke's total Conservatism is scarcely recoverable now. There is nothing climactic in Mr. Kirk's concluding chapter, 'The Recrudescence of Conservatism,' but only a confusion of ringing ambitious passages."[2] As far as the surviving Humanists and Agrarians are concerned, the banner of Conservatism has passed into other hands.*

* Chester E. Eisinger has argued that Robert Penn Warren's novels are in the tradition of Burke. It is clear that Warren is critical of the "children of light" who imagine good and evil are easily distinguished, who are too optimistic about progress, who forget the lessons of history, but Warren is not Conservative in his view of liberty and equality; he does not believe that the past is prescriptive nor does he seem ready to trade in his skepticism for a commitment to Christianity. William C. Havard, a political scientist, has been the best critic of Warren's politics. See Eisinger, *Fiction of the Forties* (Chicago, 1963), pp.

The much publicized New Conservatism is really two affiliated movements, the "libertarians," who seek to conserve the heritage of nineteenth-century Liberalism, and the "traditionalists," whose Conservatism derives from Burke and other opponents of Liberalism. The two movements have in common their opposition to social democratic tendencies in domestic politics and their determination to prosecute the Cold War to its "successful" termination. Proposals for civil rights legislation, for increased Social Security benefits, for closer diplomatic ties with the Soviet bloc —all are liable to be received wrathfully by the New Conservative of either persuasion.

Although the postwar revival of traditionalist Conservatism might be dated from Richard M. Weaver's *Ideas Have Consequences* (1948), or from Peter Viereck's *Conservatism Revisited* (1949),[3] the outstanding figure is Russell Kirk and the decisive date is 1953. In 1953, Kirk published *The Conservative Mind,* a book frequently cited in the previous chapters of this study. Kirk is an avowed, even a devout, disciple of Burke, from whom he has received the "six canons" of Conservative thought:

Belief that a divine intent rules society as well as conscience. . . . Affection for the proliferating variety and mystery of traditional life. . . . Conviction that civilized society requires orders and classes. . . . Persuasion that property and freedom are inseparably connected. . . . Faith in prescription. . . . Recognition that change and reform are not identical.[4]

By mining useful quotations from nineteenth-century British and American writers and by mounting them in richly emotive prose, Kirk moulds almost everyone he admires into the image of Burke, whom he admires most of all. The persuasiveness of this and subsequent books depends very largely on the reader. Outside the rather cloistered world of Conservatism, they seem like anthologies of homily, with little coherence and no satisfactory

198–229; Havard, "The Burden of the Literary Mind: Some Meditations on Robert Penn Warren as Historian," *South Atlantic Quarterly,* LXII (1963), 516–31.

context. Most of Kirk's books which followed *The Conservative Mind* are, in fact, collections of repetitive essays and book reviews. The titles of these collections are often highly suggestive, e.g. *Confessions of a Bohemian Tory* (1963) and *The Intemperate Professor and Other Cultural Splenetics* (1965). The chapters of the former book reveal most about the core of Kirk's thought, for in it he acknowledges his "Gothic mind, medieval in its temper and structure." [5] The phrase is apt. Although a preference for fact over theory has repeatedly been a feature of Conservative thought, Kirk himself is disposed to scholastic generalizations and, at the same time, to an almost random selection of striking illustrations. (There is certainly no evidence in his work of the quantitative empiricism which has characterized much of modern social science.) His most significant contribution after the *magnum opus* was the quarterly journal *Modern Age*, which he founded in 1955. It often prints excellent articles and reviews.

In that same year, 1955, William F. Buckley, Jr., founded *National Review*. Buckley had attended Yale and discovered a faculty committed neither to orthodox Christianity nor to laissez-faire economics. He announced this discovery to the world, especially to his fellow alumni, in an angry adolescent book—*God and Man at Yale* (1951). *National Review* is a more considerable answer to socialism within and communism without. The editors proclaimed themselves, "without reservations," on the libertarian side of the social conflicts of our time. They are "conservatives" in the relativistic sense of ordinary usage. But Kirk and other traditionalists have always been represented in the pages of the magazine.* Jeffrey Hart, celebrating the journal's tenth anniversary with his own *Festschrift,* boasts that "no important contribution by conservatives, from any country, writing in any discipline, has gone unremarked or unassimilated by the con-

---

* Prominent among contributors and editors are L. Brent Bozell, James Burnham, John Chamberlain, William Henry Chamberlain, Frank Chodorov, John Dos Passos, Max Eastman, M. Stanton Evans, Will Herberg, Willmoore Kendall, Hugh Kenner, Russell Kirk, Eugene Lyons, Frank S. Meyer, Richard Weaver, and Frederick L. Wilhelmsen.

tributors to *National Review*." [6] The claim is perhaps overstated, but the editors have been tolerant of almost anyone whose moral imagination rises to the vision implied in the following categorization:

GOOD	BAD
General Edwin Walker	*The New York Times*
Senator Joseph McCarthy	The American Association of
Senator Barry Goldwater	University Professors
racial segregation	The American Civil Liberties
The FBI	Union
wire-tapping	The Fund for the Republic
The House Committee on	Dwight Eisenhower
Un-American Activities	Chief Justice Warren
Pius XII	The Kennedy family
Chiang Kai-shek	Income tax
General Franco	Medicare
Ngo Dinh Diem	The Test-Ban Treaty
General Ky	John XXIII

There is, however, a limit to *National Review's* openness to the Right. Buckley has publicly disavowed the John Birch Society.[7]

The rhetoric is ordinarily that of nineteenth-century Liberalism, but it is hard to imagine Thomas Jefferson, John Stuart Mill, or even William Graham Sumner assessing the political situation in quite the same way as *National Review*. Many of those who proclaim the ideals of Liberalism (which they ordinarily call "conservatism") are small-town Fundamentalists whom Richard Hofstadter aptly termed the "pseudo-conservatives," whom Norman Mailer depicted at the moment of their Apocalypse (the 1964 Republican Convention that nominated Barry Goldwater):

> You could see them. . . . with their Goldwater buttons, ensconced in every lobby, a Wasp Mafia where the grapes of wrath were stored [angry, embittered, hateful, vindictive] men with high colonics and arthritis, silver-rimmed spectacles, punched-out bellies, and that air of controlled schizophrenia which is the merit badge for having spent one's life on Main Street.[8]

These are the men and women whom a combination of psychological and political-opinion tests revealed to be suspicious, rigid, compulsive, intolerant, guilty, hostile, defense, timid, frustrated, and submissive.[9]

Nonetheless, a movement ought to be judged by its best rather than by its worst representatives. Ayn Rand may be the favorite novelist of undergraduates who style themselves "conservative," but she is *persona non grata* in *National Review*. Of her, Garry Wills wrote,

> Her muscular and Malthusian heroes, the nineteenth century's messianic industrialists, the twentieth century's salvationist collectivists, are all expressions of Liberalism—the attempt to attain beatitude with a politico-economic program.[10]

Frank S. Meyer, carrying on the Liberalism which Albert Jay Nock maintained a generation ago, is perhaps the most capable of the regular contributors to the journal. He is perfectly aware of his debts to Jefferson and Mill. Although he, like a number of contributors to Rightist periodicals, once felt the appeals of communism, his reaction from Marxism is less extreme than that of many excommunists. He calls himself a conservative only because "that which is called liberalism today has deserted its heritage of defense of the freedom of the person, to become the peculiarly American form of what in Europe is called democratic socialism." [11]

Meyer is, among *National Review* regulars, the most acute critic of traditionalist Conservatism. Denying the relevance of Burke for our day, Meyer points to the fact that "history" and "tradition" can sanction almost any system—they are form rather than content.

> Either the whole historical and social situation in which [Conservatives] find themselves, including the development of collectivism, statism, and intellectual anarchy, is Providential, and all prescriptive attitudes, including the orthodox collectivist attitudes of the day, are right and true. . . . Or, there

is a higher sanction than prescription and tradition; there are standards of truth and good by which men must make their ultimate judgment of ideas and institutions; in which case, reason, operating against the background of tradition, is the faculty upon which they must depend in making that judgment.[12]

Meyer is especially caustic about the traditionalist conception of the state: "These disciples of Edmund Burke . . . believe with him that the state is a divine organ without whose positive action men cannot achieve virtue. . . ."[13] The Conservative's attack on the totalitarian state turns out to be a screen for the "subtler, quieter tyranny of 'customarily' imposed community, in which no one can escape from the deadly environment of hereditarily or geographically imposed association."[14] Most fundamentally, the Conservatives are not friends to individual liberty. They do not even understand what liberty means. Freedom is not merely freedom to do what is right. "Freedom means freedom: not necessity, but choice; not responsibility, but the choice between responsibility and irresponsibility; not duty, but the choice between accepting and rejecting duty; not virtue, but the choice between virtue and vice."[15] The phrasing often shows traces of Milton's *Areopagitica* as well as of Mill's *On Liberty:* "Virtue, which is only virtue when freely chosen . . . , is made inaccessible to the coerced citizen, wherever and to the degree that the state compels his action."[16]

Meyer has recently attempted in the introduction and in the closing essay of a very good anthology (*What is Conservatism?*) to harmonize the discordant strains of Liberalism and Conservatism, but he himself has done more than anyone else to produce the cacaphony that emanates from New Conservatism.[17] His Liberal definition of freedom was a challenge to Raymond English, who had held that the free man "is bound to try to understand and obey a system of perfect moral law," to Willmoore Kendall, who sympathized with those who put Socrates to death, and to others who have identified freedom with virtuous choice.[18] L. Brent Bozell, who had been associated with the libertarians despite his collaboration with Buckley on a book in defense of Senator McCarthy,[19] was sufficiently troubled by the freedom-virtue debate to shift his position in the direction of the traditionalists. He differed from Meyer and wrote, "The story of how the free society has come to take priority over the good society is the story of the decline of the West."[20] Reviewing *In Defense of Freedom,* Richard Weaver complained that Meyer went a "long step in the direction of Thoreau's anarchic individualism" (which Weaver had faulted in favor of John Randolph's).[21] Weaver's complaints were extravagant praise compared to the disapprobation in Kirk's review. Kirk had been Meyer's target for too many years. Now he blasted away at the "weary Liberalism" of the book, calling it "one of the most curiously unreal pieces of political pamphleteering to be produced even in this century of theoretic dogma and political fanaticism."[22] Kirk did not, in his bombast, bother to debate the issues raised.

The most impressive rebuttal to Meyer, an indirect one, came from Willmoore Kendall, whose essays in political theory are formidable efforts. Kendall had inaugurated his long campaign against Liberalism in 1941, with an assault on Locke's doctrine of majority rule, which he found to be based on the erroneous belief that popular majorities are rational, just, and informed by a true apprehension of objective moral law.[23] The real enemy was, however, John Stuart Mill, whom Kendall thought inferior to Plato.[24] "Conservatism and the 'Open Society'" ascribes to Mill the belief that *all* questions are open questions and that no proposition has a truth-value any more probable than any other proposition.[25]

Kendall does not rely on his highly theoretical "proof" of the logical errors of Liberalism; he takes the practical line as well, and insists that "No community whose members value it enough to wish to perpetuate it will submit the basic tenets of its 'dominant ethos' to untrammeled discussion by persons avowedly hostile to it. . . ." [26] On these grounds, the citizens of Holyoke, Massachusetts, had the right to silence Margaret Sanger for her views on birth control and the Congress of the United States has the right to imprison members of the Communist party.[27]

But the real interest in the freedom-virtue perplex is neither in the invectives nor in the syllogisms. It is in the common ground which the major participants seem to retire to when they have pressed each other long and hard. In a debate with M. Morton Auerbach, author of *The Conservative Illusion,* Meyer fell back to a position never occupied by Mill, Jefferson, or Spencer: "What Professor Auerbach fails to understand is that the Christian understanding of the nature and destiny of man . . . . is always and everywhere what conservatives strive to conserve." [28] In the presence of a stranger, the family squabble terminates, for this is precisely what Kendall has striven to conserve. His firmest loyalty is to the "God Whose name is Yahweh, and around Whose revelation, united in St. Paul with Greek philosophy, has grown up that which we know as Western Civilization." [29] Discussing the first volume of Eric Voegelin's *Order and History,* Kendall insisted that *"the* issue" at stake between Liberalism and Conservatism was the choice between reason and Revelation.[30] In the preface to *The Conservative Affirmation,* which is certainly a traditionalist's book, Kendall suddenly declares for the relativistic definition of "conservatism" and seems to modify his earlier views on the necessity of Christianity. He quarrels even with Meyer's answer to Auerbach. But Kendall's new model defense of that status quo seems to be derived, finally, from the religious faith which he no longer wants to bring openly into the political arena.[31]

The consensus on Christianity puts to rest the problem of freedom and virtue (at least for readers of *National Review* and *Modern Age*), but it raises another problem which is worth consideration. Buckley, in 1959, asserted that he meant to live his life "an obedient man, but obedient to God, subservient to the wisdom of my ancestors; never to the authority of political truths arrived at yesterday at the voting booth." [32] Kendall seconds Buckley:

> We believe that the proposition 'Communism is evil, and must be prevented,' is final, and final precisely because of a 'value' infinitely higher than that of 'the State'—this State, or any State. And any time the 'constitutional order' gets in our way, as regards combating the evil of Communism, we shall seek a change in the constitutional order. . . .[33]

On what grounds? For "reason of God." Kendall pushes still further and displays what must seem to a secularist an alarming readiness to give his interpretation of politics a divine sanction. What, he inquires, "if I believe *my* modicum of truth is not the expression of my finiteness but of the infinity and omniscience of God, so that in insisting upon its truthfulness for you I insist not upon my own infallibility but upon His?" [34] To those of us with less confidence in our oracular ability, the question is ominous. It is not, then, only the Marxist who threatens to appeal from established institutions to some ultimate authority that absolutizes his values, before which the decisions of ordinary politics are of little import.

The candidacy of Barry Goldwater for the presidency of the United States is quite as instructive as the muddled shuffle over virtue and freedom. The "libertarians" have been forced to emphasize the Christian basis of American society (which was not one of the Founders' main concerns); the traditionalists have, in turn, been forced by the political process to embrace a public figure whose place in the tradition of Burke is, to speak mildly, unclear.

Richard Rovere's sprightly essay, "The Minds of Barry G., or the Hazards of Catered Rhetoric," [35] shows that much of the confusion over what the senator said resulted from the fact that *The Conscience of a Conservative,* and much else of his published work, was ghost-written. Goldwater's own style is folksy and humorous in the manner of Will Rogers, but L. Brent Bozell and others have presented him "in a heavy-duty prose developed in the academy and the seminary as a vehicle for doctrinal assertion, promulgation, and dispute." [36] The point is well made, but Bozell does not seem greatly to have distorted the positions taken by Goldwater. The affable Arizonan seems sincerely to believe that the Federal government has restricted economic liberty, that the Constitution means what it says and not what the Courts say it says, and that victory is best defined as the opposite of defeat. There is a consistency in his foreign and domestic policy; both are impoverished relatives of nineteenth-century Liberalism. He seems to imagine that a peaceful world will follow "victory" over communism. He seems to believe that the liberties of the rich and powerful are threatened by the unemployed and the voteless.

If Goldwater shares Burke's sense of the past and his faith in prescription, the secret has been well kept. Nonetheless, Russell Kirk lauded him, endorsed him in 1964, and acclaimed his catastrophic defeat at the polls as a triumph for Conservatism.[37] Or for conservatism. M. Morton Auerbach's assessment is more true today than in 1959:

> Kirk is perfectly well aware that there is a difference between liberal Conservatism and conservative Liberalism. It is therefore all the more striking that his thundering denunciations of modern society should be climaxed [by] a squeaky defense of a conservative Liberal tradition no longer relevant to contemporary problems.[38]

Striking it may be, but not surprising. Conservatism is too feeble politically to stand alone and must ally itself with the conservatives. Raymond Williams perceived this and discussed the alliance in an essay on T. S. Eliot: "What is quite clear, in the New Conservatism (and this makes it very different, and much inferior to, the Conservatism of a Coleridge or a Burke) is that a genuine theoretical objection to the principle and effects of an 'atomized,' individualist society, is combined, and has to be combined, with adherence to the principles of an economic system which is based on just this 'atomized' individualist view." [39] Running for mayor of New York in 1965, William F. Buckley made equality a campaign issue—he deplored appeals to ethnic minorities, shunned the customary "balanced ticket," and refused to participate in the Columbus Day Parade. Cynics may see this as masked prejudice rather than as rationalism in politics, but the point is that Buckley was much more Liberal—rhetorically—than John Lindsay, his "Liberal" opponent.[40] To make the point more bluntly still, the followers of Burke have joined the followers of Paine in order to combat programs they imagine to originate from Marx. When the "drift" to socialism has been halted, the traditionalist Conservatives and the "libertarian" conservatives will have enough time joyfully to work out their disagreements. The day of rejoicing has, of course, been indefinitely postponed by Lyndon B. Johnson, on whom some *National Review* writers once pinned their hopes. He has turned the drift to socialism into a fairly steady course. Every step in the direction of social democracy is, of course, accompanied by shouts from the New Left: "That's not what we meant at all!" This proves not that Johnson is somehow a conservative (or even a Fascist) but that social democracy is like Liberal democracy, Conservatism, and all the other ideologies: an ideal type of social organization. The reality never has and never will be commensurate with the ideal type. That is no reason to deny improvements or—to fall back once again on Liberal rhetoric—to abandon all thought of progress.

2   *James Gould Cozzens, Realist.*

None of the New Conservatives is likely to equal the achievements of John Adams, Henry James, or George Santayana, but the novels of James Gould Cozzens are certainly comparable in quality to those of Cooper and Hawthorne. This is said not to denigrate them but to praise him. Edith Wharton, Louis Auchincloss, and J. P. Marquand have written creditable novels which scan society from the top, but Cozzens has written better ones.

His early attempts at fiction were undistinguished. Themes

from the first four novels persist, but his career is not a continous one—as he himself indicates by beginning his bibliography with his fifth book, *S. S. San Pedro,* (1931). That book is a tightly constructed, heavily symbolic novella about the death of a ship whose captain—like Herman Wouk's Captain Queeg—cannot command. There is at least the suggestion that leadership is necessary in human endeavor, but there is room for the quite opposite possibility that authority is often incompetent. The latter is not a very Conservative thought.

Ambiguity and fantasy characterize *Castaway* (1934), a restatement of the Robinson Crusoe archetype. In this version, the dream of bourgeois acquisition, security, and comfort turns nightmare when the protagonist is locked for the weekend into a department store, symbol of material abundance. He devolves into a greedy, destructive animal, a cowardly Crusoe who pursues his *Doppelgänger* to an internecine conclusion. The novel might be taken as an allegory of Original Sin; it might as easily be taken as proof that we need fear only our own unreal fears.

The Last Adam, published the year before *Castaway,* approaches the mature mode. The hero is a physician who is clearly the dominant personality in a small town in Connecticut. Chester Eisinger sees Dr. Bull as "the Conservative alive—pragmatic, responsible, aristocratic," with a strong sense of duty and a deep distrust of abstractions.[41] This interpretation imposes on the book the attitudes developed in later novels. Dr. Bull is, as his name suggests, vital, powerful, an altogether splendid fellow. He is also careless and quite irresponsible. The book's title is not—if a lonely pun is permitted—to be burked. Despite his age and his medical degree, Dr. Bull is an innocent American in the line traced by R. W. B. Lewis in *The American Adam.* Cozzens had developed his talent, discovered the milieu and written a very good book, but he could not be called a Conservative on the basis of his *oeuvre* before 1936.

In that year, Cozzens published *Men and Brethren,* which is unmistakably the kind of book he has written ever since. Although the novel is set in New York, the action is narrowly focused on the busy vicarage of the Reverend Mr. Ernest Cudlipp. Cozzens, no Christian himself, is interested in vocation and profession, in both the sacred and the profane meanings of these concepts. Cudlipp stands metaphorically at the center of a network of human needs. His telephone jangles almost constantly as he is called upon to deal with refractory bishops, with aged domestics, with naïve piety and hardened vice, with young poets and suicidal old women. In the complexity of everyday life, he exhibits "grace under pressure." He is a troubled but urbane man. He finds Karl Barth and John Calvin "wearily and long-windedly beside the point," but he is pleased to have Barth's multivolume quibbles because they set forth "a conception of religious truth which allowed modern-minded young priests . . . to recover that sustaining, snobbish ease of mental superiority, loved long since, but, fifty or sixty years ago, lost to the clergy for a while." When pressed for a statement of faith, he simply recites his Church's creed: "I believe in one catholic and apostolic church. . . ." His faith is reinforced by a mundane sense of the intractability of facts. In this world, one does what one can, and "realists are the only people who get things done. A realist does the best he can with things as they are. Don't waste your time trying to change things so you can do something." Knowing the deviousness of human motives, he can answer queries about his own—he became a priest, he says, because it was the easy way out and because it was God's will.

Ernest Cudlipp has arrived at a maturity which Abner Coates, hero of *The Just and The Unjust* (1942), reaches at that novel's conclusion.* Abner Coates is the Assistant District Attorney of a small Massachusetts town. While involved in a murder trial, he is approached by the political boss of the town, who asks him to run for District Attorney. Since he is the son and grandson of es-

* *Ask Me Tomorrow,* published (1940) between *Men and Brethren* and *The Just and The Unjust,* is an autobiographical novel about a failed writer. It falls below the level of *The Last Adam* and subsequent books.

teemed judges, the offer is attractive. His decision and the jury's are two parts of the same lesson in life's intricacy.

After careful deliberation, Abner decides to accept the nomination—because he needs the money to marry, because his ambition requires the post, because he thinks he can do a better job than the Democratic candidate, because it would be foolish to turn down the chance.

After somewhat less rational deliberation, the jury comes to its decision. Abner knows that juries, like other organized groups, "often showed a collective apprehension and a collective way of reasoning that transcended the individual's reasoning and disregarded the individual's logic." He also knows that theory and practice are two distinct matters, but his comprehension of this wisdom is too intellectual. When the jury comes to what is obviously the wrong verdict, Abner is disappointed. He is, however, too experienced to be overwhelmed. He resolves to use his prospective mite of power as justly as he can, for right action is "the one real pleasure, when all was said and done, of power." He continues to believe in the law which is, in his grandfather's summary, "the stronghold of what reason men ever get around to using." The wise man does not scorn the useful because it is imperfect. Abner's father advises him, in another complicated case, to do what's legal and not to worry about what is, in some abstract ethical sense, just. Philander Coates, aged realist, has the last word:

> The world gets up in the morning and is fed and goes to work, and in the evening it comes home and is fed again and perhaps has a little amusement and goes to sleep. To make that possible, so much has to be done by so many people that, on the face of it, it is impossible. Well, every day we do it; and every day, come hell, come high water, we're going to have to go on doing it as well as we can.

A novelist as Conservative as Cozzens was surely destined to write of military as well as of civilian institutions. The hero of *Guard of Honor* (1948) is a judge summoned back to uniform in

World War II. Lawyer and soldier, he is a Conservative understood and affirmed.

The central crisis in *Guard of Honor* turns on the question of race relations. A hotheaded veteran punches a Negro flier who had inadvertently endangered the lives of the hothead, his commander (General Beal), and Colonel Ross, the novel's hero. The crisis, inaccurately reported by the press, is intensified when incompetent Colonel Mowbray, following Southern custom, bars Negro airmen from the Officers' Club. Tensions are made more taut by the suicide of an officer shunted off to a minor command, by petty troubles among the Wacs, by the death of paratroops dropped into a lake left unpatrolled by the crash boat supposedly on guard.

Through all this, General Beal lives an unquestioned code—the Military Academy's Duty-Honor-Country:

> It probably never crossed [his] mind that . . . books had been written to show that Country was a delusive projection of the individual's ego; and that there were men who considered it the part of intelligence to admit that Honor was a hypocritical social sanction protecting the position of a ruling class; or that Duty was self-interest as it appeared when sanctions like Honor had fantastically distorted it.

Colonel Ross differs from General Beal mainly in that he is conscious of the role he plays, aware of the criticisms made of his ideals. He moves in World War II, as he had in World War I, from the institutions appropriate in peacetime (the law) to those appropriate in wartime (the army). Although excluded from the "mystic order" of West Pointers, he is nonetheless an "old Army man." He accepts the military as it is because he accepts the world as it is. Standing with General Beal to review formations of men and planes, acting out the ceremonies of military life, Colonel Ross thinks of Biblical wisdom ("Oft He seems to hide His face, but unexpectedly returns . . .") and formulates his creed: "A man must stand up and do the best he can with what there is."

His conservative philosophy is summed up in the four lines of Pope that come to him as he stands in thought:

> All Nature is but art unknown to thee;
> All chance, direction, which thou canst not see;
> All discord, harmony not understood;
> All partial evil, universal good.

This philosophy is challenged by Lieutenant Edsell, a Marxist who asserts that the state is "the product of class antagonisms and the instrument of class domination." Edsell distorts the conflict: "The unreconstructed Confederates and other poor white trash, some of it from West Point, got all hot and bothered" and "decided to strike a blow for White Supremacy." Lieutenant Edsell proposes to do something about the "sadistic sub-morons down in dear old Dixie." He introduces into the already confused scene the father of the assaulted airman and a reporter from the Negro press.

Colonel Ross rebukes both Lieutenant Edsell and Colonel Mowbray. He handles the racial crisis with common sense (truckle now, profit later) and with legalistic compromise (the Club is off limits not for Negroes but for "temporary personnel," all of whom are Negroes). He helps cover the blunders of Colonel Mowbray, whose failure to note the reported breakdown of the crash boat doomed the paratroops. He holds the fort while General Beal flies himself together. (Flight calms the general.) He insists on a guard of honor for the self-slain officer:

> It does us good. Ceremony is for us. The guard . . . of honor
> is a suitable mark of our regret for mortality and our respect
> for service—we hope, good; but if bad or indifferent, at least,
> long. When you are as old as I am you will realize that it
> ought to get a man something. For our sake, not his. Not
> much; but something. Something people can see.

Colonel Ross was not the last of Cozzens's lawyer heroes. He returned in *By Love Possessed* (1957) to a more thorough exploration of the territory mapped out in *The Just and The Unjust*. Although Dwight Macdonald and other critics have lampooned Cozzens for the Jamesian lushness of his prose and for the Adams-like bareness of his politics,[42] the novel is still a very good one.

The story begins with Arthur Winner, Jr., visiting his mother and ironically contemplating an old French gilt clock on which is written *omnia vincit amor*. Arthur is a lawyer in his fifties, old enough to smile at such romanticism, experienced enough to emulate his lawyer father. Arthur Winner, Sr., had been "the Man, if not perfectly, at least predominantly, of Reason," the man who knew very well that Christianity is a "venerated fable," who supported the church nonetheless, as a center of social stability.

The complications of Arthur Winner's day defy synopsis—one of the main points of mature Cozzens is that our diurnal course is more involved than that of rocks and stones and trees. The major lines of the plot concern a finished but unforgotten love affair between Arthur Winner and Marjorie Penrose, some funds held in trust by the senior member of his law firm, the difficulties of Helen and Ralph Detweiler, and the political ambitions of District Attorney J. Jerome Brophy. The lines are tangled. Helen Detweiler, the law firm's secretary, lost her parents years before, revolted against her own survival, and devoted herself to her worthless brother Ralph; in the course of the novel, she commits suicide because Ralph reveals himself to be a petty thief as well as an irresponsible fornicator. J. Jerome Brophy is involved because he intercedes in Ralph's arrest on a charge of alleged rape. His appeal to Arthur Winner not to run for office against him raises an obvious conflict of interest. The mismanaged funds and the quondam love affair are also related. The misuse of money by Noah Tuttle, the most upright lawyer in the community, is uncovered by Arthur Winner, who protests to Julius Penrose, the third member of the partnership. Julius argues that Noah should be protected—after all, he's paid back part of the $200,000 involved. Arthur is indignantly legalistic until Julius lets him know that he, Julius, has known all along about the old affair between his wife and Arthur. The moment is comparable to moments in the late novels of Henry James:

> If you knew of something that you believed I didn't know, and that you thought it better I should not know, I'm persuaded you'd do as much for me—try every way to keep it from me. . . . Let me be more explicit. I'm persuaded, Arthur, that you *have* done as much for me. And, if unknown to you, I've always thanked you for it.

The lesson of the master is the familiar one. Ideals can never be perfectly institutionalized in a world of imperfect men. The law is a "science as inexact as medicine, [which] must do its justice with the imprecision of wisdom, the pragmatism of a long, a mighty experience." It was, as Blackstone had long ago observed, a "mysterious science."

Arthur Winner understands this, acquiesces in the discreet silence about Noah Tuttle's malfeasance, and visits his mother once again. Once again he observes the old gilt clock with the youthful motto. He answers her call: "He said: 'I'm here.'" There is no final victory, there is only co-existence with daily uncertainties. There is no ultimate truth, there is only the wisdom of our fathers, passed on to us in the institutions they fashioned. We are free to do the best we can with what we have.

3   *The Present and the Future*

From the days of Jonathan Boucher and Governor Hutchinson to those of Russell Kirk and James Gould Cozzens, Conservatism has had its American proponents. Few of them have accepted all the tenets of the political faith of Edmund Burke or of Leo XIII, but many of our most important writers have responded to the dream of an orderly, disciplined, hierarchical society inwardly formed by a sense of the past. It is highly unlikely that the dream can be realized, but, on the other hand, few dreams are. It is in the nature of politics that ideologies are never completely institutionalized. The question, for anyone interested in Conservatism, is this: Of what relevance is the Conservative imagination today? What can Conservatives contribute to a new synthesis of American ideals?

The complex of processes political scientists call modernization shows no sign of reversal. Isolated individuals turn to primitivism and to handicrafts, but all nations seem anxious for an industrial infrastructure—even when they have no need for many of the projects in which they invest their capital and their pride. Technology seems to advance in geometrical progression. Society becomes ever more bureaucratic. The displaced and dispossessed of the Radical Right are not likely to call off their anguished hunt for the conspiracy which has done them in, but neither are the Minute Men and the Birchers likely to recover the lost world of William Graham Sumner.

The conservative Liberals, i.e. the "libertarians," have much to warn against but little to offer. Like the invention of the wheel, which many nomads must have looked upon as a sign of "dehumanization," nuclear and electronic developments have socially negative as well as socially positive consequences. The "libertarians" are surely right to value freedom, but if freedom is to survive it will be within the institutional structures of a social system organized and computerized beyond the dreams of science fiction.

Social democracy, which sees in technological change a chance to achieve equality of opportunity (and not just to assume it), is more likely to increase freedom for all than Liberal democracy, which has, historically, enlarged the freedom of the middle class against the few above and the many below. The political and economic power of the men who style themselves "conservative" is, of course, far more impressive than the ideology of the National Association of Manufacturers or the Southern wing of the Democratic party, but the political tendency since 1933 has weakened that power considerably.

The economic sector, which is often the only one in which the "libertarians" advocate decrease of governmental power, has moved into a new stage as distinct from corporate capitalism as that oligopolistic stage was from the individual ownership of private property described by John Locke. Modern capitalism is so vastly different from the market-centered activity of the nineteenth century that the word "capitalism" no longer describes the contemporary economic system. The degree of government intervention in the planned economies of Europe and the United States is so great that Andrew Shonfield, in his brilliant book on modern capitalism,[43] is tempted to seek another word. (He settles for concept plus adjective.)

But what of the traditionalists, of the true Conservatives whose change from politics into literature has been the main subject of this book? It is hard to imagine that their decline will not continue, but it is possible to hope that certain aspects of Conservatism can be incorporated into the pragmatic form of social democracy that has become the status quo.*

One of these aspects is a sense of community and of social obligation. Fraternity is a greater ideal than community because the brotherhood of man is a nobler concept than the kinship of any smaller group, but the sorry truth is that the globe is divided among a hundred nations, each claiming the right to conscript its citizens and send them off to kill the citizens of other nations, or to die in the attempt.† The dream of the parliament of man is unrealized, and the disintegration of smaller collectivities, under the constant pressure of modernization, produces a mixed lot of

* Although my primary concern here is with political ideals and not with empirical description of contemporary societies, I think it worthy of note that some of today's foremost political scientists and sociologists have argued that traditionalist elements strengthen rather than weaken democratic society. Predemocratic elements tend to keep the system pluralistic. See William Kornhauser, *The Politics of Mass Society* (New York, 1959), and Gabriel Almond and Sidney Verba, *The Civic Culture* (rev. ed., Boston, 1965).

† I recognize that values derive from human preferences. I assume that no reader wants to have this bit of relativism inserted grammatically into every sentence.

blessings and curses. The Conservative, at his best, understands that the quality of an individual's life is inextricably bound to the quality of the society in which he lives.

One need not be a Conservative to feel that the life of a modern city is not what it should be. The most optimistic of us must have qualms when people stand in crowds to watch a murderer pursue his victim or urge a neurotic to jump from a skyscraper. Racial strife may be the result of social injustice, but social injustice in a nation as rich as ours is itself a sign of the collapse of a community. As John Kenneth Galbraith noted, private interests flourish and public facilities decay. This selfishness destroys community more slowly but as surely as mob violence.

In our time, communities have disintegrated on the national as well as on the local level. One modern society—Germany—was transformed into a machine to exterminate its own citizens. Another—Spain—died in civil war. Traditional communities are anachronisms, but the idea of community is implicit in modern socialisms, in Fabianism as well as Marxism.

Social democracy, including fraternity among its ideals, has often achieved communal solidarity, or at least, in Europe, a kind of class solidarity. In our time, radicals like Paul Goodman have cooperated with Conservatives like Robert Nisbet in the quest for community.[44] But the sense of the past is *not* an element in Marxism, in Fabianism, or in the American compromise dubbed "modern Liberalism." Liberal democracy and social democracy are both oriented toward the future; neither is ready yet to indulge in that sense of the past which is fundamental to Conservative thought.

Rejection of Burke's belief in prescription is necessary, but ignorance of the past is—in technical jargon—socially dysfunctional. The past is *instrumentally* instructive in that it aids us in understanding the present and future. Most Liberals and socialists would grant this. But the past is also *humanely* instructive. Conservatism reminds us that no one genuinely interested in the humanities can be easy with the modern tendency to imagine that the metamorphoses of art are somehow comparable to the advancement of science, that technological proficiency implies moral superiority. We cannot be easy at the thought of a generation unmoved by the world of the Greek *polis,* uninterested in the Biblical myths that were more real to the American Puritans than the wilderness they lived in, bored by Shakespeare, blind to Michelangelo, and deaf to Mozart. Rationality must be conceived broadly, humanistically, after the example of George Santayana, if the efficient production of goods and services is not to mean the onset of social amnesia. The Conservative insists that Conservatism alone preserves human diversity and achievement. The problem for social democracy is not only to assure everyone the material basis for a good life but also to expand, preserve, and make available for all men the diverse, priceless achievements of the past as well as the present. This is not an impossible goal, and there are signs that American culture, in the narrower sense of the term, is closer now than fifty years ago to the ideal of the Humanists.

In an age of advertiser-financed mass media, it is difficult to act upon Matthew Arnold's dictum that we value the best that has been thought and said. It is more difficult still to feel the value of a past that has *not* been prized by some sort of *consensus gentium,* but there is, nonetheless, a joy in continuity as well as in inauguration. There is a pride in preservation as well as in creation. Thinking of his native Salem in the preface to *The Scarlet Letter,* Hawthorne described the "old wooden houses, the mud and dust, the dead level of site and sentiment, the chill east wind, and the chillest of social atmospheres," but he went on to acknowledge that "the spell survives, and just as powerfully as if the natal spot were an earthly paradise." He condemned the past and departed from home, but he always returned "as if Salem were for me the inevitable centre of the universe." We need not be Conservatives to understand him.

It seems unlikely that a people uninterested in its origins—however inglorious they may be—can respond fully to its present, or worry intelligently about its future. We may not be ready—as Henry James *was*—to suggest that the sense of the past is the basis of all that is valuable in our lives, but James was right to feel that sense to be an indispensable part of civilized existence. "Socialism," wrote Irving Howe and Lewis Coser, "is the name of our desire." [45] Encouraged by the fact that their epigram is an amendment of Tolstoy, I should like to amend them: socialism with a sense of the past is the name of my desire. To state a goal is not, of course, to attain it, but the prerequisite for its attainment is to be clear about directions, to know the name of our desires.

Notes

INTRODUCTION *Liberalism and the Political Theory of Edmund Burke*

1 Louis Hartz, *The Liberal Tradition in America* (New York, 1955), p. 57. See also Hartz, *The Founding of New Societies* (New York, 1964), pp. 1–23, 69–122.

2 Samuel P. Huntington, "Conservatism as an Ideology," *American Political Science Review*, LI (1957), 455.

3 Willmoore Kendall, *The Conservative Affirmation* (Chicago, 1963), p. ix. Simply because this *is* the customary usage in popular speech, a hundred additional citations could be added.

4 Friedrich von Hayek, *The Constitution of Liberty* (Chicago, 1960), pp. 397–8.

5 W. A. Kerr, "Untangling the Liberalism-Conservatism Continuum," xxxv (1952), 111–25.

6 A conflict of definitions makes a shambles of *Conservatism, Liberalism, and National Issues*, ed. by Lee S. Greene for the *Annals of the American Academy of Political and Social Science*, cccxliv (1962).

7 Auerbach defines conservatism in terms of harmony and tranquillity. "Conservative harmony requires the minimizing of individual desires and the maximizing of affection through a 'community,' integrated by traditions and institutions handed down from the past." See M. Morton Auerbach, *The Conservative Illusion* (New York, 1959), p. 1.

8 For Kissinger, see "Conservative Dilemma: Reflections on the Political Thought of Metternich," *American Political Science Review*, xlviii (1954), 1017–30; for Viereck, see *Conservatism Revisited* (New York, 1949).

9 For a discussion of Catholic Conservatism, see pp. 80–92.

10 See Max Weber, *The Theory of Social and Economic Organization*,

ed. Talcott Parsons (New York, 1964), pp. 100–12; Maurice Duverger, *Political Parties* (London, 1954), pp. xiii–xiv.

11 See Frank Petrella, "Edmund Burke: A Liberal Practitioner of Political Economy," *Modern Age*, VIII (1963–1964), 52–60.

12 Ernest Barker, *Essays on Government*, 2nd ed. (Oxford, 1951), pp. 231–3. I do agree with Barker's judgment.

13 Alfred Cobban, *Edmund Burke and the Revolt against the Eighteenth Century* (London, 1929), p. 88.

14 Barker, *Essays on Government*, p. 219.

15 Peter J. Stanlis, *Edmund Burke and the Natural Law* (Ann Arbor, 1958), p. 83; see also Francis P. Canavan, *The Political Reason of Edmund Burke* (Durham, 1960). For a disagreement on this matter, see C. B. MacPherson, "Edmund Burke and the New Conservatism," *Science and Society*, XXII (1958), 231–9.

16 Clinton Rossiter, *Conservatism in America*, 2nd ed. (New York, 1962), p. 234.

17 Russell Kirk, *A Program for Conservatives* (Chicago, 1954), p. 32; Willmoore Kendall and George W. Carey, "Towards a Definition of 'Conservatism,'" *Journal of Politics*, XXVI (1964), 420. See also Arnold A. Rogow, "Edmund Burke and the American Liberal Tradition," *Antioch Review*, XVII (1957), 255–65. On the other side, See Auerbach, *The Conservative Illusion*, p. 146; Bernard Crick, "The Strange Quest for an American Conservatism," *Review of Politics*, XVII (1955), 359–76; Ludwig Freund, "New American Conservatism and European Conservatism," *Ethics*, LXVI (1955), 10–17; Elisha Greifer, "Conservative Pose in America," *Western Political Quarterly*, XV (1962), 5–16; Robert A. Nisbet, "Conservatism and Sociology," *American Journal of Sociology*, LVIII (1952), 167–75; Eric McKitrick "'Conservatism' Today," *American Scholar*, XXVII (1957–1958), 49–61; Francis G. Wilson, "The Anatomy of Conservatives," *Ethics*, LXX (1960), 265–81.

18 See Daniel Aaron, "Conservatism, Old and New," *American Quarterly*, VI (1954), 99–110; Phillip C. Chapman, "The New Conservatism: Cultural Criticism v. Political Philosophy," *Political Science Quarterly*, LXXV (1960), 17–34; Richard Chase, "Neo-Conservatism and American Literature," *Commentary*, XXIII (1957), 254–61; Peter Viereck, *The Unadjusted Man* (Boston, 1956), p. 90.

19 Kirk's *The Conservative Mind* (Chicago, 1952) is not the exception it seems because (1) Kirk labels nearly everyone he likes a Conservative and (2) he displays an inadequate comprehension of American social and economic history.

20 See Auerbach, *The Conservative Illusion;* David Spitz, *Patterns of*

Anti-Democratic Thought (New York, 1949), and Spitz, *Essays in the Liberal Idea of Freedom* (Tucson, 1964), Part III.

I *The Decline of American Conservatism*

1 R. R. Palmer, *The Age of the Democratic Revolution,* 2 vols. (Princeton, 1959–1964), I, 188.

2 Wallace Brown, *The King's Friends: The Composition and Motives of the American Loyalist Claimants* (Providence, 1965), p. 3. See also Leonard Woods Labaree, *Conservatism in Early American History* (New York, 1948) and William H. Nelson, *The American Tory* (Oxford, 1961).

3 Carl Becker, *Political Parties in New York, 1760–1766.* (Madison, 1909). In addition to Becker, writers stressing revolutionary consequences of the war are A. M. Schlesinger, "The American Revolution Reconsidered," *Political Science Quarterly,* xxxiv (1919), 61–78; J. Franklin Jameson, *The American Revolution Considered as a Social Movement* (Princeton, 1926); Merrill Jensen, "Democracy and the American Revolution," *Huntington Library Quarterly,* xx (1957), 321–41; Jackson Turner Main, "Government by the People: The American Revolution and the Democratization of the Legislatures," *William & Mary Quarterly,* 3rd Series, xxiii (1966), 391–407. Among the revisionists are Oscar and Mary Handlin, "Radicals and Conservatives in Massachusetts after Independence," *New England Quarterly,* xvii (1944), 343–55; Frederick B. Tolles, "The American Revolution Considered as a Social Movement: a Re-Evaluation," *American Historical Review,* lx (1954), 1–12; Robert E. Brown, *Middle-Class Democracy and the Revolution in Massachusetts* (Ithaca, 1955).

4 Russell Kirk, *The Conservative Mind,* p. 71. See also Daniel Boorstin, *The Genius of American Politics* (Chicago, 1953), pp. 80–98.

5 Palmer, *The Age of the Democratic Revolution,* I, 188–9.

6 Nelson, *The American Tory,* p. v.

7 Quoted in Moses Coit Tyler, *The Literary History of the American Revolution,* 2nd ed., 2 vols. (New York, 1957), I, 319.

8 Vernon Parrington, *Main Currents in American Thought,* 3 vols. (New York, 1927–1930), I, 215.

9 Jonathan Boucher, *A View of the Causes and Consequences of the American Revolution,* p. xv.

10 Ibid. pp. 310–11.

11 Ibid. p. 498.

12 Ibid. pp. 509, 511.

13 Ibid. p. 546.

14 Ibid.

15 Ibid. pp. 514-15.

16 Thomas Hutchinson, *The History of the Colony and Province of Massachusetts-Bay*, ed. Lawrence Shaw Mayo, 3 vols. (Cambridge, Mass., 1936), I, 66.

17 Ibid. pp. 35-6.

18 Ibid. pp. 311, 328.

19 Ibid. II, 219.

20 Ibid. III, 293-4.

21 Quoted in James K. Hosmer, *The Life of Thomas Hutchinson* (Boston, 1896), p. 189.

22 Parrington, *Main Currents in American Thought*, pp. 195, 203.

23 Nelson, *The American Tory*, p. 3.

24 Hannah Arendt, *On Revolution* (New York, 1963), pp. 179-215.

25 Clinton Rossiter, *1787: The Grand Convention* (New York, 1966), p. 148.

26 Joseph Charles, *The Origins of the American Party System* (Williamsburg, 1956), p. 4. See also Arendt, *On Revolution*, p. 110.

27 Palmer, *The Age of the Democratic Revolution*, II, pp. 54-5.

28 *The Works of John Adams*, ed. Charles Francis Adams, 10 vols. (Boston, 1850-1856), III, 449.

29 Ibid. p. 453-4.

30 Ibid. IV, 219-20.

31 Ibid. p. 216.

32 Ibid. IV, 293.

33 Ibid. p. 292.

34 Ibid. VI, 220.

35 Ibid. IX, 563.

36 For Washington's views, see Louis Martin Sears, *George Washington and the French Revolution* (Detroit, 1960).

37 Quoted in Zoltán Haraszti, *John Adams and the Prophets of Progress* (Cambridge, Mass., 1952), p. 92.

38 Ibid. p. 257.

39 Diary entry for August 9, 1770, in *The Adams Papers*, ed. L. H. Butterfield, *Series I: Diaries*, 4 vols. (Cambridge, Mass., 1961), I, 360.

40 *The Adams-Jefferson Letters*, ed. Lester J. Cappon, 2 vols. (*Chapel Hill*, 1959), II, 397-402.

41 John Adams, *Works*, IV, 290, 354-5, 392, 398, 414.

42 Quoted in Haraszti, *John Adams and the Prophets of Progress*, p. 201. See also Manning Dauer, *The Adams Federalists* (Baltimore, 1953),

p. 55, and John R. Howe, Jr., *The Changing Political Thought of John Adams* (Princeton, 1966), Chapter 6.

43 Edward Handler, *America and Europe in the Political Thought of John Adams* (Cambridge, Mass., 1964), p. 60.

44 Randall B. Ripley, "Adams, Burke, and Eighteenth-Century Conservatism," *Political Science Quarterly,* LXXX (1965), 216–35.

45 Haraszti, *John Adams and the Prophets of Progress,* p. 48.

46 *The Adams-Jefferson Letters,* II, 456.

47 *Alexander Hamilton and the Founding of the Nation,* ed. Richard B. Morris (New York, 1957), pp. 9, 15.

48 Ibid. p. 124.

49 See Broadus Mitchell, *Alexander Hamilton,* 2 vols. (New York, 1957–1962), II, 466–8, on the one side, and Julian Boyd, *No. 7: Alexander Hamilton's Secret Attempts to Control American Foreign Policy* (Princeton, 1964), on the other.

50 Clinton Rossiter, *Alexander Hamilton and the Constitution* (New York, 1964), p. 162.

51 William Nisbet Chambers, *Political Parties in a New Nation* (New York, 1963), pp. 58–9.

52 Hutchinson, *The History of the Colony and Province of Massachusetts-Bay,* II, 160.

53 Jonathan Jackson, *Thoughts upon the Political Situation* (Worcester, Mass., 1788), p. 58.

54 Ibid. p. 158.

55 See the second of the *Camillus* letters, published in the *Independent Chronicle* of 1787, reprinted in *The Works of Fisher Ames,* ed. Seth Ames, 2 vols. (Boston, 1854), II, 104.

56 Ibid. p. 212.

57 Ibid. p. 221; see also p. 82.

58 Winifred E. A. Bernhard, *Fisher Ames: Federalist and Statesman* (Chapel Hill, 1965), p. 354.

59 For an excellent collection, see Lewis Simpson, *The Federalist Literary Mind* (Baton Rouge, 1962).

60 David Hackett Fischer, "The Myth of the Essex Junto," *William & Mary Quarterly,* 3rd Series, XXI (1964), 199.

61 As Fischer notes in his book, (*The Revolution of American Conservatism* (New York, 1965), p. xviiin), the conventional view has the sanction of three authorities: Shaw Livermore, Jr., *The Twilight of Federalism* (Princeton, 1962); William Nisbet Chambers, *Political Parties in a New Nation;* and Seymour M. Lipset, *The First New Nation* (New York, 1963).

62 Fischer, *The Revolution of American Conservatism*, p. 153.

63 Ibid. p. 109.

64 Samuel Eliot Morison, *Life and Letters of Harrison Gray Otis*, 2 vols. (Boston, 1913), I, 49.

65 C. R. King, *The Life and Correspondence of Rufus King*, 6 vols. (New York, 1894–1900), V, 535.

66 Wilbert E. Moore and Robin M. Williams, "Stratification in the Ante-Bellum South," *American Sociological Review*, VII (1942), 344.

67 Eugene D. Genovese, *The Political Economy of Slavery* (New York, 1965), p. 23.

68 Barrington Moore, Jr., *The Social Origins of Dictatorship and Democracy: Lord and Peasant in the Making of the Modern World* (Boston 1966), pp. 116, 123.

69 Stanley Elkins, *Slavery: A Problem in American Institutional and Intellectual Life* (Chicago, 1959). The capitalistic aspects of Southern life are brilliantly illuminated from an unusual angle in David Bertelson, *The Lazy South* (New York, 1967), which shows that the alleged "indolence" of Southern life was often the energetic private pursuit of goals not openly related to public ends.

70 See Arnold A. Sio, "Interpretations of Slavery: The Slave Status in the Americas," *Comparative Studies in Society and History*, VII (1965), 289–308; David Brion Davis, *The Problem of Slavery in Western Culture* (Ithaca, 1966), pp. 223–61.

71 See Fletcher M. Green, "Democracy in the Old South," *Journal of Southern History*, XII (1946), 3–23.

72 See Stanley Elkins and Eric McKitrick, "A Meaning for Turner's Frontier: Part II," *Political Science Quarterly*, LXIX (1964), 565–602.

73 W. J. Cash, *The Mind of the South* (New York, 1941), p. 37.

74 Russell Kirk, *Randolph of Roanoke* (Chicago, 1951), p. 19.

75 The letter was to John Hay, 3 September 1882, *Letters of Henry Adams*, ed. Worthington Channcey Ford (Boston, 1930), p. 338. The biography was published in the same year.

76 Norman K. Risjord, *The Old Republicans* (New York, 1965), p. 3.

77 Quoted in Charles M. Wiltse, *John C. Calhoun*, 3 vols. (Indianapolis, 1944–1951), I, 337–8.

78 Ibid. II, 71.

79 John C. Calhoun, *A Disquisition on Government*, ed. C. Gordon Post (New York, 1953), pp. 3–4.

80 Ibid. p. 11. This is, of course, one of the rights which Burke denied.

81 Ibid. p. 7.

82 Ibid. p. 20.

83 Wiltse, *John C. Calhoun*, I, 270–71.

84 Quoted in George M. Frederickson, *The Inner Civil War* (New York, 1965), p. 132.

85 See Jesse T. Carpenter, *The South as a Conscious Minority* (New York, 1930), pp. 221–60.

86 Louis Hartz, *The Liberal Tradition*, pp. 145–77.

87 C. Vann Woodward, Introduction to George Fitzhugh, *Cannibals All!* (Cambridge, Mass., 1960), p. viii.

88 George Fitzhugh, *Sociology for the South* (Richmond, 1854), p. 175.

89 Ibid. p. 69.

90 Fitzhugh, *Cannibals All!*, p. 69.

91 Charles Grier Sellers, Jr., "The Travail of Slavery," in Sellers, *The Southerner as American* (Chapel Hill, 1960) p. 64.

92 On the novel's origin as a bourgeois and representational mode, see Ian Watt, *The Rise of the Novel* (Berkeley, 1957).

93 William R. Taylor, *Cavalier and Yankee: The Old South and American National Character* (New York, 1961), p. 184. For a similar judgment, see Bertelson, *The Lazy South*, pp. 184–6.

94 Quoted by Taylor, *Cavalier and Yankee*, p. 324.

95 See especially, "Americanism in Literature," *Views and Reviews in American Literature*, ed. C. Hugh Holman (Cambridge, 1962), pp. 7–29.

96 Taylor, *Cavalier and Yankee*, p. 17.

II *Images of Value and a Sense of the Past*

1 Henry S. Canby, *Classic Americans: A Study of Eminent American Writers from Irving to Whitman* (New York, 1931), p. 86; Henry A. Pochmann, *Washington Irving: Representative Selections* (New York, 1934), p. xlv.

2 William L. Hedges comes to many of the same conclusions in his excellent book, *Washington Irving: An American Study* (Baltimore, 1965), pp. 164–90.

3 See Sir Lewis Namier, *England in the Age of the American Revolution* (London, 1930), pp. 15–20.

4 Henry Nash Smith, *Virgin Land* (Cambridge, Mass., 1950); R. W. B. Lewis, *The American Adam* (Chicago, 1955); Leo Marx, *The Machine in the Garden* (New York, 1964).

5 Quoted in Pierre M. Irving, *Life and Letters of Washington Irving*, 4 vols. (New York, 1862–1863), I, 441.

6 Washington Irving, *The Crayon Miscellany: A Tour of the Prairies,* IX, 9, 53. *Astoria,* written largely from the papers of John Jacob Astor, is an account of the bitter hardships of Western exploration and settlement.

7 An excellent essay on Jonson's poem and its Conservatism is Jeffrey Hart, "Ben Jonson's Good Society," *Modern Age,* VII (1963), 61–8.

8 Pierre M. Irving, *Life and Letters of Washington Irving,* IV, 167.

9 Philip Young, "Fallen From Time; The Mythic Rip Van Winkle," *Kenyon Review,* XXII (1960), 547–73. See also Terence Martin, "Rip, Ichabod, and the American Imagination," *American Literature,* XXXI (1959), 137–49.

10 Daniel Hoffman, *Form and Fable in American Fiction* (New York, 1961), p. 89.

11 Quoted in Thomas Philbrick, "Cooper's *The Pioneers:* Origins and Structure," *PMLA,* LXXIX (1964), 582. This is to my knowledge the best essay on *The Pioneers.*

12 On William Cooper, see Robert E. Spiller, *Fenimore Cooper: Critic of His Times* (New York, 1931), chap. 2.

13 Robert Zoellner, "Conceptual Ambivalence in Cooper's Leatherstocking," *American Literature,* XXXI (1960), 397–420.

14 James Fenimore Cooper, *The Bravo* (1831), *The Heidenmauer* (1832), and *The Headsman* (1833). For a good discussion of these three, see Marius Bewley, *The Eccentric Design* (New York, 1959), pp. 48–64.

15 For the ins and outs of Cooper's politics, and a correction of earlier accounts, see Dorothy Waples, *The Whig Myth of James Fenimore Cooper* (New Haven, 1938).

16 On the late novels, see Donald A. Ringe, *James Fenimore Cooper* (New York, 1962), pp. 115–44, and A. N. Kaul, *The American Vision* (New Haven, 1963), pp. 84–138.

17 Views similar to my own can be found in Roy R. Male, *Hawthorne's Tragic Vision* (Austin, Texas, 1957) p. 41: "If a study of the house as symbol in American literature were undertaken, certainly one conclusion would be that the home has consistently represented, whether consciously or not, an attempt to build an integrated, functioning religious experience: a fusion of time and space, investment and speculation, past and present." See also Norman Holmes Pearson, *The American Writer and the Feeling for Community* (University, Alabama, 1962).

18. Roy Harvey Pearce, "Hawthorne and the Sense of the Past," *ELH,* XXI (1954), 327–49; Marvin Fisher, "The Pattern of Conservatism in Johnson's *Rasselas* and Hawthorne's Tales," *Journal of the History of Ideas,* XIX (1958), 173–96; Pearce, "Romance and the Study of History," *Hawthorne Centenary Essays,* ed. Roy Harvey Pearce (Columbus, Ohio,

1964), pp. 221–44; Christoph Lohmann, "The Burden of the Past in Hawthorne's Romances," *South Atlantic Quarterly,* LXVI (1967), 92–104.

19 On the relationship to England, see Lawrence S. Hall, *Hawthorne: Critic of Society* (New Haven, 1944), chap. 4.

20 *Hawthorne's Dr. Grimshawe's Secret,* ed. Edward H. Davidson (Cambridge, Mass., 1954), pp. 146–7. See also Davidson, *Hawthorne's Last Phase* (New Haven, 1949).

21 *The Letters of Henry James,* ed. Percy Lubbock, 2 vols. (New York, 1920), I, 13.

22 Henry James, *Essays in London and Elsewhere* (New York, 1893), pp. 6–7.

23 Quoted in Ernest Samuels, *Henry Adams: The Middle Years* (Cambridge, Mass., 1958), p. 127.

24 Almost every "Jacobite" has discussed the international theme. Specifically devoted to the subject are Christof Wegelin, *The Image of Europe in Henry James* (Dallas, 1958) and Alan Holder, *Three Voyagers in Search of Europe* (Philadelphia, 1966).

25 The phrase appears in a letter to H. G. Wells, 10 July 1915, in *Letters,* II, 490.

26 Henry James, *The American Scene* (New York, 1907), p. 12.

27 Preface to *The Aspern Papers.*

28 On the mixture of comic and tragic in James, see Richard Poirier, *The Comic Sense of Henry James* (London, 1960).

29 Nor is it enough in America, as James makes plain in *The Bostonians,* a marvelous novel which takes off from Hawthorne's *Blithedale Romance.* Architectural metaphors are important in most of James, but especially in *The Spoils of Poynton* and *Washington Square.* James and Edith Wharton are discussed in James W. Tuttleton, "Henry James and Edith Wharton: Fiction as the House of Fame," *Midcontinent American Studies Journal,* VII (1966), 25–36.

30 The review is reprinted in Howells, *Criticism and Fiction* (1891), and also in *Discovery of a Genius: William Dean Howells and Henry James,* ed. Albert Mordell (New York, 1961), pp. 92–7.

31 The quoted terms are from the unhappy letter James sent back to Howells, 31 January 1880, *Letters,* I, 72.

32 For an excellent analysis of class and status in the novel, see Kermit Vanderbilt, "Howells among the Brahmins," *New England Quarterly,* XXXV (1962), 291–317.

33 Quoted in Edwin H. Cady, *The Realist at War* (Syracuse, 1958), p. 44.

34 See Hyatt Waggoner, *William Faulkner: From Jefferson to the*

World (Lexington, Ky., 1959); Cleanth Brooks, *William Faulkner: The Yoknapatawpha Country* (New Haven, 1963). Of all the books on Faulkner, I find Olga Vickery's most helpful: *The Novels of William Faulkner* (Baton Rouge, La. 1959).

35   The quoted phrases are from Stevens's "A Postcard from the Volcano."

III   *The Establishment of Religion*

1   Russell Kirk, *The Conservative Mind* (3rd ed., Chicago, 1960), p. 7; Samuel P. Huntington, "Conservatism as an Ideology," *American Political Science Review,* LI (1957), 456; Clinton Rossiter, *Conservatism in America*, p. 42.

2   For a valuable discussion, see E. V. Walter, "Conservatism Recrudescent: A Critique," *Partisan Review,* XXI (1954), 518–19. Walter quotes Martin Buber's *Between Man and Man* (p. 77): "No legitimate use can be made in politics or political theory of the concept of human sinfulness."

3   Edmund Burke, "Speech on the Petition of the Unitarians," *Works,* VII, 43.

4   Ernest Barker, *Essays on Government,* pp. 224–7; Peter J. Stanlis, *Edmund Burke and the Natural Law,* pp. 195–230; Carl B. Cone, *Burke and the Nature of Politics,* 2 vols. (Lexington, Ky., 1957–1964), II, 285–8.

5   Joseph de Maistre, *Works,* ed. Jack Lively (New York, 1965), pp. 106, 108.

6   For a rather optimistic survey of the Protestant churches, see Winthrop Hudson, *The Great Tradition of the American Churches* (New York, 1953).

7   Jonathan Boucher, *A View of the Causes and Consequences of the American Revolution,* pp. 103–4.

8   *Travels in New-England,* 4 vols. (New Haven, 1821–1822), IV, 401.

9   Zoltán Haraszti, *John Adams and the Prophets of Progress,* p. 329.

10   Arthur M. Schlesinger, Jr., *Orestes A. Brownson* (Boston, 1939). For typical essays by Catholics, see Virgil Michel, "Brownson: A Man of Men," *Catholic World,* CXXV (1927), 755–62; M. A. Fitzsimons, "Brownson's Search for the Kingdom of God," *Review of Politics,* XVI (1954), 22–36; Paul Conroy, "The Role of the American Constitution in the Political Philosophy of Orestes A. Brownson," *Catholic Historical Review,* XXV (1939), 271–86. A significant exception to the trend is Kirk's introduc-

tion to a collection of essays, reprinted in *Beyond the Dreams of Avarice* (Chicago, 1956), pp. 133–52.

11   See Francis E. McMahon, "Orestes Brownson on Church and State," *Theological Studies,* xv (1954), 175–228; Orestes A. Brownson, "The Works of Fisher Ames," *Brownson's Quarterly Review,* 3rd Series, 11 (1854), 502–14; Tayler Lewis, *A Discourse on the True Idea of the State* (Andover, 1843), pp. 6n-7n. Joseph L. Blau has a good essay on this interesting minor figure, "Tayler Lewis, True Conservative," *Journal of the History of Ideas,* xiii (1952), 218–33.

12   Orestes A. Brownson, "Democracy," *Boston Quarterly Review,* 1 (1838), 67.

13   Brownson, "Slavery—Abolitionism," *Boston Quarterly Review,* 1 (1838), 257.

14   Brownson, "Religion and Politics," *Boston Quarterly Review,* 1 (1838), 322, 332.

15   Brownson, "Democracy and Christianity," *Boston Quarterly Review,* 1 (1838), 464.

16   Brownson, *Boston Quarterly Review,* iii (1840), 385. First of two parts.

17   Brownson, "Democracy and Liberty," *Democratic Review,* xii (1843), 374.

18   Ibid. p. 382.

19   Ibid. p. 387.

20   Ibid. p. 386.

21   Brownson, "Origin and Ground of Government," *Democratic Review,* xiii (1843), 252.

22   Brownson, "Authority and Liberty," *Brownson's Quarterly Review,* N.S., iii (1849), 150.

23   Ibid. pp. 155–6.

24   Brownson, "Origin and Ground of Government," *Democratic Review,* xiii (1843), 374.

25   Father Stanley J. Parry, C.S.C., "The Premises of Brownson's Political Theory," *Review of Politics,* xvi (1954), 209. Father Parry is also one of the contributors to Frank S. Meyer's collection, *What Is Conservatism?* (New York, 1964). Another excellent article is A. Robert Caponigri, "Brownson and Emerson: Nature and History," *New England Quarterly,* xviii (1945), 368–90.

26   Parry, "The Premises of Brownson's Political Theory," p. 210.

27   Brownson, "Catholicity Necessary to Sustain Popular Liberty." *Brownson's Quarterly Review,* ii (1845), 514–30. See also James Rowland,

"Brownson and the American Republic Today," *Catholic World,* CLII (1941), 537–41.

28   Brownson, *The American Republic* (New York, 1866), p. 428.

29   Ibid. pp. 429, 439.

30   Theodore Maynard, *Orestes Brownson* (New York, 1943), p. 233. Rossiter, in *Conservatism in America,* ends his chapter on "The Conservative Minority" with a brief discussion of the Conservatism of Roman Catholic political theory (pp. 232–4).

31   Henry J. Browne, "Catholicism in the United States," *The Shaping of American Religion,* ed. James Ward Smith and A. Leland Jamison (Princeton, 1961), p. 115.

32   Robert D. Cross, *The Emergence of Liberal Catholicism in America* (Cambridge, Mass., 1958).

33   See Anson Phelps Stokes, *Church and State in the United States,* 3 vols. (New York, 1950), I, 330; John Tracy Ellis, *Perspectives in American Catholicism* (Baltimore, 1963), pp. 2–3.

34   James Cardinal Gibbons, "The Church and the Republic," *North American Review,* CLXXXIX (1909), 336.

35   Number 55 in the Syllabus of Errors. Number 80 condemns the proposition that "The Roman Pontiff can, and ought to, reconcile himself and come to terms with progress, liberalism, and modern civilization."

36   See *Testem Benevolentiae* (1899). A great controversy has grown up about the letter, addressed to Cardinal Gibbons about a heresy in France traced to American statements of doubtful orthodoxy attributed to Father Isaac Hecker. The standard study is Thomas McAvoy, *The Great Crisis in American Catholic History* (Chicago, 1957).

37   James Cardinal Gibbons, "The Church and the Republic," pp. 335–6.

38   Father Francis J. Connell, "Christ the King of Civil Rulers," *American Ecclesiastical Review,* CXIX (1948), 245, 252.

39   An excellent summary and expansion of Murray's position can be found in Richard Regan, S.J., *American Pluralism and the Catholic Conscience* (New York, 1963), pp. 38–71.

40   Father George W. Shea, "Catholic Doctrine and 'The Religion of the State,'" *American Ecclesiastical Review,* CXXIII (1950), 161–74.

41   Father Joseph Fenton, "The Status of a Controversy," *American Ecclesiastical Review,* CXXIV (1951), 458.

42   Victor Yanitelli, "Chronicle: A Church-State Controversy," *Thought,* XXVI (1951), 443–51; Connell, "The Theory of the 'Lay State,'" *American Ecclesiastical Review,* CXXV (1951), 7–18; Murray, "For the Freedom and Transcendence of the Church," *American Ecclesiastical Review,* CXXVI

(1952), 28–48; Connell, "Reply to Father Murray," *American Ecclesiastical Review*, cxxvi (1952), 49–59.

43 Alfredo Cardinal Ottaviani, "Church and State," *American Ecclesiastical Review*, cxxviii (1953), 321–34.

44 The American Conservative's unhappiness with John xxiii is the subject of Garry Wills, *Politics and Catholic Freedom* (Chicago, 1964).

45 The two essays on James are reprinted in Edmund Wilson, *The Shock of Recognition* (New York, 1943), pp. 854–65. On the line from Hawthorne to Eliot, see F. O. Matthiessen's great book, *American Renaissance* (New York, 1941), pp. 351–68.

46 T. S. Eliot, *Complete Poems and Plays* (New York, 1952), p. 43.

47 Ibid. p. 21. The poem is "Gerontion."

48 Eliot, *Selected Essays* (2nd American ed., New York, 1950), pp. 6–7.

49 Eliot, "Religion and Literature," *Selected Essays*, p. 343.

50 Eliot, *For Lancelot Andrewes: Essays on Style and Order* (Garden City, N.Y., 1929), pp. vii, 55.

51 Eliot, *The Use of Poetry and the Use of Criticism* (London, 1933), pp. 41–2. It is no surprise that Eliot in this book defended Catholic and communist censorships as correct in principle, p. 136n.

52 Eliot, "A Commentary," *Criterion*, x (1931), 481–90.

53 In 1940, in "Literature and the Modern World," he wrote, "When society is conceived as merely the sum of individuals, you get the chaos of liberal democracy." See *America Through the Essay*, ed. A Theodore Johnson and Allen Tate (New York, 1940), p. 382.

54 Eliot, *After Strange Gods: A Primer of Modern Heresy* (New York, 1934), p. 20.

55 Ibid. p. 66.

56 On Lawrence, see my essay, "D. H. Lawrence: The Politics of Irrationality," *Wisconsin Studies in Contemporary Literature*, v (1964), 151–63.

57 Eliot, "A Commentary," *Criterion*, xiii (1934), 629.

58 Eliot, *Complete Poems and Plays*, p. 187.

59 Ibid. p. 206.

60 Ibid. p. 221.

61 Eliot, *The Idea of a Christian Society* (New York, 1940), p. 27.

62 Ibid. pp. 51–2.

63 Ibid. p. 46.

64 Eliot, *Notes towards the Definition of Culture* (New York, 1949), p. 126.

65 Ibid. p. 47.

66 Eliot, *On Poetry and Poets* (New York, 1957), p. 72.

67   Not sanguinely. See Russell Kirk *Confessions of a Bohemian Tory* (New York, 1963), p. 217.

68   Kirk, *The Conservative Mind,* 3rd ed., pp. 551–2.

IV   Conservatism and the Military Establishment

1   Quoted phrases are from J. Frank Dobie, "Samples of the Army Mind," *Harper's,* cxciii (1946), 529–36; "The U.S. Military Mind," *Fortune,* xlv (February 1952), 91–3, 202, 204, 206, 208; Fred J. Cook, *The Warfare State* (New York, 1962), pp. 7, 351; C. Wright Mills, *The Causes of World War III* (New York, 1958); Tristram Coffin, *The Passion of the Hawks* (New York, 1964), p. 244; and John M. Swomley, Jr., *The Military Establishment* (Boston, 1964). For an analysis of the semantic disarray of most attacks, see Lewis J. Edinger, "Military Leaders and Foreign Policy-Making," *American Political Science Review,* lvii (1963), 392–405.

2   Samuel P. Huntington, *The Soldier and the State* (Cambridge, Mass., 1959), p. vii.

3   Ibid. p. 90.

4   For the original version of Lasswell's concept, see "The Garrison State," *American Journal of Sociology,* xlvi (1941), 455–68. Lasswell's second thoughts are to be found in "The Garrison-State Hypothesis Today," *Changing Patterns of Military Politics,* ed. Samuel P. Huntington (Glencoe, Ill., 1962), pp. 51–70.

5   Huntington, *The Soldier and the State,* p. 79.

6   Ibid. p. 64.

7   Ibid. p. 462.

8   Ibid. p. 463.

9   For selected essays on *Billy Budd* and a bibliographic guide to other essays, see *Melville's Billy Budd and the Critics,* ed. William T. Stafford (Belmont, California, 1961).

10   E. L. Grant Watson, "Melville's Testament of Acceptance," *New England Quarterly,* vi (1933), 319–27.

11   Huntington, *The Soldier and the State,* p. 465. Huntington does not cite Ralph Adams Cram in his book, but Huntington surely responded as West Point's builder meant him to. See Cram's *The Ministry of Art* (Boston, 1914), pp. 204–8.

12   Douglas MacArthur, *Reminiscences* (New York, 1964), pp. 423, 425–6.

13   Morris Janowitz, *The Professional Soldier* (Glencoe, Ill., 1960), p. 21. See also *The New Military,* ed. Morris Janowitz, (New York, 1964);

Gene M. Lyons, "The New Civil-Military Relations," *American Political Science Review,* LV (1961), 53–63.

14 Jonathan M. Wainwright, *General Wainwright's Story* (Garden City, N.Y., 1946), pp. 298–9.

15 *The Stilwell Papers,* ed. Theodore H. White (New York, 1948), p. 60.

16 Ladislas Farago, *Patton: Ordeal and Triumph* (New York, 1964), p. 94; George S. Patton, *War As I Knew It* (Boston, 1947), pp. 18–19.

17 L. K. Truscott, Jr., *Command Missions* (New York, 1954), p. 75.

18 Mark W. Clark, *Calculated Risk* (New York, 1950), pp. 114–15.

19 Ibid. p. 130.

20 Huntington, *The Soldier and the State,* p. 267.

21 Quoted in Courtney Whitney, *MacArthur: His Rendezvous with Destiny* (New York, 1956), p. 492.

22 Huntington, *The Common Defense* (New York, 1961), p. xii.

23 Aron, *Peace and War: A Theory of International Relations,* trans. Richard Howard and Annette Baker Fox (Garden City, N.Y., 1966), p. 132.

24 William T. Sherman, *Memoirs,* 2 vols. (New York, 1887), II, p. 111.

25 Quoted in Janowitz, *The Professional Soldier,* p. 268.

26 Omar N. Bradley, *A Soldier's Story* (New York, 1951), p. xi.

27 MacArthur used the phrase more than once. The most famous occasion was his Address to the Joint Session of Congress, 19 April 1951, reprinted in *Reminiscences,* pp. 400–405.

28 The most influential titles are probably Hans J. Morgenthau, *Politics among Nations* (New York, 1949); George Kennan, *American Diplomacy, 1900–1950* (Chicago, 1951); and Robert E. Osgood, *Ideals and Self-Interest in America's Foreign Relations* (Chicago, 1953).

29 The incident takes place in Book V, Chapter 89 of Thucydides' history of the Peloponnesian War. For an analysis of the difference between foreign and domestic policy and an argument similar to the one here, see Stanley Hoffmann, *The State of War* (New York, 1965).

30 Aron, *Peace and War: A Theory of International Relations,* p. 329.

31 Quoted in Haraszti, *John Adams and the Prophets of Progress,* p. 205.

32 MacArthur, *Reminiscences,* p. 80.

33 Robert K. Merton, *Social Theory and Social Structure* (2nd ed., Glencoe, Ill., 1957), p. 195. On the difference between the ascribed status of traditional hierarchy and the achieved status of military organization, see Janowitz, *Sociology and the Military Establishment* (New York, 1959), chap. 2; for a fascinating account of functional hierarchy's replacement of

hierarchy based on civilian standards, see Robert C. Stone, "Status and Leadership in a Combat Flight Squadron," *American Journal of Sociology,* LI (1946), 388–94.

34   Dwight D. Eisenhower, *Crusade in Europe* (Garden City, N.Y., 1948), p. 477.

35   James M. Gavin, *War and Peace in the Space Age* (New York, 1958), p. 253.

36   Matthew B. Ridgway, *Soldier* (New York, 1956), p. 98.

37   Huntington, "Power, Expertise, and the Military Profession," *Daedalus,* XCII (1963), 804. On the very different attitudes of the younger officers, see Richard W. Van Wagenen, "American Defense Officials' Views on the U.N.," *Western Political Quarterly,* XIV (1961), 104–19.

38   Samuel Stouffer *et al., The American Soldier,* 2 vols. (Princeton, 1949), I, 55.

39   The best critique is by Hans Speier, "The American Soldier and the Sociology of Military Organization," *Continuities in Social Research,* ed. Robert K. Merton and Paul F. Lazarsfeld (Glencoe, Ill., 1950), pp. 106–32.

40   Representative of the first group of studies are Arnold Rose, "The Social Structure of the Army," *American Journal of Sociology,* LI (1946), 361–4; Howard Brotz and Everett Wilson, "Characteristics of Military Society," *American Journal of Sociology,* LI (1946), 371–5; Arthur K. Davis, "Bureaucratic Patterns in the Navy Officer Corps," *Social Forces,* XXVII (1948), 143–53; Felton D. Freeman, "The Army as a Social Structure," *Social Forces,* XXVII (1948), 78–83; and G. Dearborn Spindler, "The Military—a Systematic Analysis," *Social Forces,* XXVII (1948), 83–8.

41   See Donald T. Campbell and Thelma M. McCormack, "Military Experience and Attitudes toward Authority," *American Journal of Sociology,* LXII (1957), 482–90; E. P. Hollander, "Authoritarianism and Leadership Choice in a Military Setting," *Journal of Abnormal and Social Psychology,* XLIX (1954), 365–70; and Andrew F. Henry and Edgar E. Borgatta, "A Comparison of Attitudes of Enlisted and Commissioned Air Force Personnel," *American Sociological Review,* XVIII (1953), 669–71.

42   Janowitz, *The Professional Soldier,* p. 92.

43   Mark W. Clark, *From The Danube to the Yalu* (New York, 1954), p. 199.

44   It is no surprise, for instance, to discover that the military have behaved better than local police in race riots. See Allen D. Grimshaw, "Actions of Police and the Military in American Race Riots," *Phylon,* XXIV (1963), 271–89.

45   Janowitz, *The Professional Soldier,* p. 243.

46   Ibid. pp. 254–5.

47   MacArthur, *Reminiscences,* p. 417.

V.   *The Revival of Conservative Ideas*

1   Barrington Moore, Jr., *The Social Origins of Dictatorship and Democracy,* pp. 111–55.

2   George M. Frederickson, *The Inner Civil War,* p. 164.

3   Quoted by Matthew Josephson, *The Robber Barons* (New York, 1934), p. 50.

4   Ibid. p. 72.

5   Charles Francis Adams and Henry Adams, *Chapters of Erie and Other Essays* (Boston, 1871), p. 2.

6   Ibid. p. 95.

7   Ibid. p. 134. *The Law of Civilization and Decay,* by Brooks Adams, continues the family quarrel with finance capitalism, but at a much lower intellectual level.

8   The witticism is from *The Education of Henry Adams* (Boston, 1918), p. 266.

9   *Letters of Henry Adams,* p. 284.

10   See, for the comparison of Boston and Geneva, J. C. Levenson, *The Mind and Art of Henry Adams* (Boston, 1957), pp. 22–3.

11   Henry Adams, *The Life of Albert Gallatin* (2nd ed., New York, 1943), p. 266.

12   Henry Adams, *History of The United States of America During the Administrations of Thomas Jefferson and James Madison,* 9 vols. (New York, 1889–91), I, 185.

13   Ibid. I, 213.

14   Ibid. I, 217.

15   Ibid. I, 30.

16   Ibid. I, 31.

17   Ibid. VIII, 146–7.

18   On Adams's relation to the thirteenth century, see Michael Colacurcio, "The Dynamo and the Angelic Doctor: The Bias of Henry Adams' Medievalism," *American Quarterly,* XVII (1965), 696–712.

19   In addition to Chapter XXIII of the *Education,* see *The Degradation of the Democratic Dogma,* ed. Brooks Adams (Boston, 1919), pp. 263–311. The standard study of the theory of history is William Jordy, *Henry Adams: Scientific Historian* (New Haven, 1952).

20   Ernest Samuels, *Henry Adams: The Middle Years* (Cambridge,

Mass., 1958), pp. 155, 271; and Samuels, *Henry Adams: The Major Phase* (Cambridge, Mass., 1964), pp. 263, 559.

21 *A Cycle of Adams Letters,* ed. Worthington Chauncey Ford, 2 vols. (Boston, 1920), I, 282.

22 Kirk, *The Conservative Mind* (London, 1954), p. 318.

23 Irving Babbitt, "Humanism: An Essay at Definition," *Humanism and America,* ed. Norman Foerster (New York, 1930), p. 28; *Literature and the American College* (Boston, 1908), p. 7.

24 Harry Hayden Clark, one of the Humanists, calls Babbitt and More "Burkean Federalists" in "A Democratic Aristocrat," *American Review,* II (1933), 240.

25 Babbitt, *Literature and the American College,* p. 74.

26 Babbitt, *The New Laokoon* (Boston, 1910), p. 198.

27 Babbitt, *Democracy and Leadership* (Boston, 1924), pp. 294, 298.

28 Allen Tate "The Fallacy of Humanism," *Criterion,* VIII (1929), 678.

29 Babbitt, *On Being Creative* (Boston, 1932), p. xxxiv.

30 Paul Elmer More, *On Being Human* (Princeton, 1936), p. 37. George Roy Elliott's tribute to Babbitt contains the same lament. *Humanism and Imagination* (Chapel Hill, 1938), pp. 23–45.

31 More, *Shelburne Essays, 1st Series* (New York, 1906), p. 1.

32 More, *Shelburne Essays, 7th Series* (New York, 1910), p. 191

33 More, *The Drift of Romanticism* (Boston, 1913), p. 255. See also the title essay of *The Demon of the Absolute* (Princeton, 1928).

34 More, *The Drift of Romanticism,* p. 282.

35 More, *Aristocracy and Justice* (Boston, 1915), p. 14.

36 Ibid. pp. 36–7.

37 Ibid. p. 136.

38 Ibid. p. 116.

39 More, *A New England Group and Others* (Boston, 1921), pp. 93–4.

40 Ibid. p. 123.

41 More, *The Greek Tradition,* 6 vols. (Princeton, 1921–31), III, 293.

42 Quoted in Arthur Hazard Dakin, *Paul Elmer More* (Princeton, 1960), p. 290.

43 Russell Kirk, *The Conservative Mind,* p. 375.

44 Quoted in Dakin, *Paul Elmer More,* p. 367.

45 This view is clearest in Ralph Adams Cram, *Gold, Frankincense and Myrrh* (Boston, 1919).

46 Cram, *Convictions and Controversies* (Boston, 1935), p. 9.

47 The best statement of the theory of history is in Cram, *The Great Thousand Years* (Boston, 1918).

48 Cram, *The Ruined Abbeys of Great Britain* (New York, 1905), p. 283.

49 Cram, *The Sins of the Fathers* (Boston, 1919), p. 98.

50 The description of community is in Cram, *Walled Towns;* the quotation comes from his *The Nemesis of Mediocrity* (Boston, 1917), p. 39.

51 For the architecture, see Cram, *My Life in Architecture* (Boston, 1936).

52 George Santayana, *The Works of George Santayana,* 14 vols. (New York, 1936–37), II, chap. 8.

53 Santayana, *Works,* I, 87–8.

54 Santayana, *The Middle Span* (New York, 1945), p. 35.

55 Santayana, *Works,* I, viii.

56 Santayana, *The Middle Span,* p. 169.

57 Santayana, *Dominations and Powers* (New York, 1951), p. vii.

58 Santayana, *Works,* IX, 175.

59 Ibid. p. 178.

60 Santayana, *Dominations and Powers,* p. 60.

61 Santayana, *Works,* IX, 166.

62 Santayana, *Works,* III, 303–4.

63 Ibid. p. 289.

64 Ibid. p. 314.

65 Ibid. p. 298.

66 Ibid. p. 319.

67 Santayana, *Works,* II, 228.

68 Kirk, *The Conservative Mind,* p. 384.

69 Santayana, *Works,* II, 285.

70 Ibid. II, 23.

71 Richard C. Lyon, "Santayana and the Real Thing," *Shenendoah,* XVII (1966), 55.

72 Santayana, *Works,* I, 205.

73 See Lyon, "Santayana and the Real Thing," p. 48.

74 Santayana, *Works,* X, 195.

75 Santayana, *Works,* III, 262.

76 Santayana, *Letters,* ed. Daniel Cory (New York, 1955), p. 35.

77 Herbert Schneider, *A History of American Philosophy* (New York, 1946), p. 414.

78 Norman Foerster, *Humanism and America* (New York, 1930).

79 Allen Tate, "Last Days of the Charming Lady," *Nation,* CXXI (1925), 485–6.

80 Tate, "Where Are the People?," *American Review,* II (1933), 234; Donald Davidson, *I'll Take My Stand,* 2nd ed. (New York, 1962), p. 35.

81 Ibid. p. 95.

82　For an account of the magazine, see Albert E. Stone, Jr., "Seward Collins and the *American Review*," *American Quarterly*, XII (1960), 3–19.

83　Andrew Lytle, *I'll Take My Stand*, pp. 201–45.

84　Davidson, *"I'll Take My Stand: A History," American Review*, V (1935), 309.

85　See Tate, "What Is a Traditional Society?," *American Review*, VII (1936), 376–87.

86　Quoted in Louise Cowan, *The Fugitive Group* (Baton Rouge, 1959), p. 242.

87　Alan Swallow reissued the novel with an introduction by Arthur Mizener which has, in turn, been reprinted in *The Sense of Life in the Modern Novel* (Boston, 1964).

88　Tate, *Jefferson Davis: His Rise and Fall* (New York, 1929), p. 301.

89　*I'll Take My Stand*, p. 171.

90　Ibid. pp. 1, 3.

91　Ibid. p. 5.

92　John Crowe Ransom, *The World's Body* (New York, 1938), p. 42.

93　Tate, *Stonewall Jackson: The Good Soldier* (New York, 1928), p. 39.

94　Tate, *Jefferson Davis*, p. 43.

95　Ibid. p. 87.

96　Ibid. p. 45.

97　Ransom, *God Without Thunder* (2nd ed., Hamden, Conn., 1965), p. 327.

98　Robert Gorham Davis, "The New Criticism and the Democratic Tradition," *American Scholar*, XIX (1949–50), 9–19.

99　An amusing critique of this group is Kathleen Nott's *The Emperor's Clothes* (Bloomington, Ind., 1954).

100　Theodore Karanikas, *Tillers of the Myth: Southern Agrarians as Social and Literary Critics* (Madison, Wis., 1966), p. 198.

101　Ransom, *The World's Body*, p. 41.

102　Ibid. p. 42.

103　See Max Weber, *The Theory of Social and Economic Organization*, pp. 88–115.

104　Eliot, *For Lancelot Andrewes*, p. 49n.

105　Eliot, "Tradition and the Individual Talent," *Selected Essays*, p. 4.

VI　*The Present and the Future*

1　See Donald Davidson, *Still Rebels, Still Yankees* (Baton Rouge, 1957); Cleanth Brooks, *William Faulkner: The Yoknapatawpha Country* (New Haven, 1963).

2   Ransom, "Empirics in Politics," *Poems and Essays* (New York, 1955), p. 144.

3   Viereck is an exception to the generalization about Conservatism and social democracy. See his *Conservatism Revisited* (New York, 1949), pp. 16–17; *Shame and Glory of the Intellectuals* (Boston, 1953) p. 62; *The Unadjusted Man* (Boston, 1956).

4   Kirk, *The Conservative Mind*, pp. 17–18.

5   Kirk, *Confessions of a Bohemian Tory* (New York, 1963), p. 23. Other titles are *Randolph of Roanoke* (Chicago, 1951); *A Program for Conservatives* (Chicago, 1954); *Academic Freedom* (Chicago, 1955); *Beyond the Dreams of Avarice* (Chicago, 1956); *The American Cause* (Chicago, 1957); *The Intelligent Woman's Guide to Conservatism* (New York, 1957); *Old House of Fear*, a novel (New York, 1961); *The Surly Sullen Bell*, a book of stories (New York, 1962); and *The Intemperate Professor* (Baton Rouge, 1965).

6   Jeffrey Hart, *The American Dissent: A Decade of Modern Conservatism* (New York, 1966), pp. 15–16.

7   See "The Question of Robert Welch," *National Review*, xii (February 13, 1962), 83–8.

8   Hofstadter's essay first appeared in the *American Scholar* (1955). It was reprinted in Daniel Bell's collection, *The New American Right* (1955) and in the revised edition of that book (with a postscript) in 1963. The original essay, the postscript, and an essay on "Goldwater and Pseudo-Conservative Politics" all appear in Part I of Hofstadter's *The Paranoid Style in American Politics* (New York, 1965). For Mailer's essay, which originally appeared in *Esquire* (November 1964), see *Cannibals and Christians* (New York, 1966), pp. 1–45.

9   Herbert McClosky, "Conservatism and Personality," *American Political Science Review*, lii (1958), 27–45. The same volume contains replies by Willmoore Kendall and Morton Frisch, pp. 506–10, 1108–11.

10   "But Is Ayn Rand Conservative?," *National Review*, viii (February 27, 1960), 139. See also Whittaker Chambers, "Big Sister Is Watching You," *National Review*, iv (December 28, 1957), 594–6.

11   Frank S. Meyer, *In Defense of Freedom* (Chicago, 1962), p. 1.

12   Ibid. p. 41.

13   Ibid. p. 133. See also Leo Strauss, *Natural Right and History* (Chicago, 1953), pp. 318–19.

14   Meyer, *In Defense of Freedom*, p. 141.

15   Ibid. p. 53.

16   Meyer, "Why Freedom," *National Review*, xiii (September 25, 1962), 223.

17   Meyer, *What Is Conservatism?* (New York, 1964), chaps. 1 and 13.

18 Raymond English, "Of Human Freedom," *Modern Age*, III (1958–59), 8–20; Willmoore Kendall, "The People Versus Socrates Revisited," *Modern Age*, III (1958–59), pp. 98–111.

19 L. Brent Bozell and William F. Buckley, Jr., *McCarthy and His Enemies* (Chicago, 1954).

20 Bozell, "Freedom or Virtue?," *National Review*, XIII (September 11, 1962), 206.

21 Richard Weaver, "Anatomy of Freedom," *National Review*, XIII (December 4, 1962), 444.

22 For one of Meyer's early assaults on Kirk, see "In Defense of John Stuart Mill," *National Review*, I (March 28, 1956), 23–4. For Kirk's review, see "An Ideologue of Liberty," *Sewanee Review*, LXXII (1964), 349–50. An account of the dispute appears in Hart, *The American Dissent: A Decade of Modern Conservatism*, pp. 213–23.

23 Willmoore Kendall, *John Locke and the Doctrine of Majority-Rule* (Urbana, 1941).

24 See note 18, above. The most important work on Mill's side of the Plato-versus-Mill controversy is, of course, Karl Popper, *The Open Society and Its Enemies* (Princeton, 1950).

25 Kendall, *The Conservative Affirmation*, pp. 100–120.

26 Ibid. p. 202.

27 Ibid. pp. 195–210, 218–20.

28 Meyer, "Do-It-Yourself Conservatism?," *National Review*, XII (January 30, 1962), 59.

29 Kendall, *The Conservative Affirmation*, p. 145.

30 Ibid. p. 242.

31 For similar regressions to religious grounds, see Father Stanley J. Parry, C.S.C., "Reason and the Restoration of Tradition," *What Is Conservatism?*, pp. 107–29.

32 Buckley, *Up from Liberalism* (New York, 1959), p. 203.

33 Kendall, *The Conservative Affirmation*, p. 220.

34 Ibid. p. 147.

35 The essay is reprinted in Richard Rovere, *The Goldwater Caper* (New York, 1965).

36 Ibid. p. 43.

37 The most egregious of Kirk's essays is "The Mind of Barry Goldwater," *Confessions of a Bohemian Tory*, pp. 185–92. This follows "A Conversation with the Infanta," a discussion with Carlist royalty. The announcement of Conservatism's victory in 1964 can be found in "New Direction in the U.S.: Right?," *The New York Times Magazine*, August 7, 1966.

38   Auerbach, *The Conservative Illusion*, p. 153.

39   Raymond Williams, "Second Thoughts: T. S. Eliot on Culture," *Essays in Criticism*, VI (1956), 317–18.

40   See Buckley, *The Unmaking of a Mayor* (New York, 1966).

41   Chester Eisinger, *Fiction of the Forties*, p. 158. Eisinger's analysis is, on the whole, a perceptive one. On the Conservative in Cozzens, see also Frederick Bracher, *The Novels of James Gould Cozzens* (New York, 1959), chap. 1; and John Lydenberg, "Cozzens and the Conservatives," *Critique*, 1 (1958), 3–9.

42   Dwight Macdonald, "By Cozzens Possessed," *Commentary*, xxv (1958), 36–47.

43   Andrew Shonfield, *Modern Capitalism: The Changing Balance of Public and Private Power* (London, 1965).

44   Paul and Percival Goodman, *Communitas* (New York, 1960); Robert A. Nisbet, *The Quest for Community* (New York, 1953).

45   Irving Howe and Lewis Coser, "Images of Socialism," in Irving Howe, *A World More Attractive* (New York, 1963), p. 227.

Index